BAO
& DIM SUM

ORATHAY SOUKSISAVANH
PHOTOGRAPHY BY CHARLOTTE LASCÈVE

BAO
& DIM SUM

Hardie Grant

BOOKS

IN MY CHINESE KITCHEN

我的中式廚房

When I was two years old, every day at the same time I would take my rocking chair out onto the patio and wait for my father to come home. My mother – still bewildered to this day – continues to wonder where I got this firm grasp of time. Five minutes later, there was my father, bearing a bag containing two steaming hot bao buns. And so the ritual would begin . . . I would rip open the first bun and gobble up the filling. Then I would grab hold of the second bun and devour the filling of that one too.

Afterwards, I used to stare at the white dough left in the bag. Diligently, I finished up the buns bit by bit, one mouthful at a time. Two bao buns, every day at snack time, at two years of age! Later, I had a kitten called Bao.

We cooked a lot in our house, from morning until night, but we never used to make dumplings. They were a treat reserved for family meals out.

That was our Sunday lunchtime outing, instead of church. Rather than celebrating mass, we would reel off the numbers of the dishes we wanted to order to the waiter. Har gao, xiu mai, char siu bao . . . these names punctuated my childhood years.

It wasn't until much later, when I began writing cookery books, that I started badgering my mother to test out all sorts of recipes. Recipes we loved eating but never made ourselves. These are the recipes I wanted to put down in writing as part of our family's culinary heritage, and which I am sharing with you now.

Orathay Souksisavanh

MENU
BAO & DIM SUM

CHOOSING THE RIGHT
INGREDIENTS

FOR BAO BUNS

You don't need any unusual or costly ingredients to make the pastry for bao buns. So, treat yourself instead to a high-quality organic strong white bread flour to enhance the flavour. The same goes for the sugar: choose unrefined sugar if possible. And sift the flour for optimum lightness.

FOR DIM SUM

You don't need any special ingredients for dim sum made with wheat flour.

STARCH

WHEAT STARCH (1): to make starch-based dumplings (which are slightly translucent), you will need starch or wheat starch (wheat flour without the gluten). Once cooked, pastry made using this type of starch is white and translucent.

TAPIOCA STARCH (2): derived from manioc, tapioca starch has a completely neutral flavour. It is very popular in Asian cooking thanks to the texture and elasticity it gives dishes. Combining these two types of starch therefore allows you to make soft pastry with a slight resistance.

READY-MADE PASTRY

WONTON PASTRY (3): square pastry wrappers made with wheat flour and egg. They could be described as the Chinese cousin of Italian ravioli: wonton means 'dumpling' in Cantonese. You will find this type of pastry in the chilled foods section of Asian grocery stores, next to the noodles and fresh pasta. Mainly used for soup dumplings, fried dumplings and cork-shaped dumplings (*xiu mai*). This pastry can also be used for making Italian ravioli filled with cheese, foie gras or duck breast fillet.

GYOZA PASTRY (4): round pastry wrappers used for making gyozas (Japanese dumplings). Albeit of Chinese origin, the pastry is distinguished by its thinness. It is egg-free and made with flour, starch and water. You will find it in the frozen food section of Asian grocery stores, and sometimes in the fresh food section of Japanese stores.

PEKING DUMPLING PASTRY: nowadays, you can buy discs of pastry for making Peking dumplings, used in the same way as gyoza pastry wrappers. You will find it in the fresh food section of some grocery stores, next to the wonton pastry wrappers.

GROCERIES AND SAUCES

You can get most of the basic ingredients you need (soy sauce, oyster sauce, dried shiitake mushrooms (5), wood ear mushrooms (6)) in ordinary supermarkets. I still recommend taking a stroll around Asian grocery stores though.

Water chestnuts: diced and mixed with meat, they add a little crunch and freshness to the filling. They are sold in tins. They can be substituted with carrot or kohlrabi, but not with exactly the same effect. Freeze any leftovers in a small bag.

Chinese five spices or 5-spice powder: not to be confused with four spices. This is a Chinese blend containing cinnamon, star anise, Sichuan pepper, fennel seeds and coriander (cilantro). It sometimes also contains orange peel and liquorice. Goes very well with stewed meat and duck. Sold in small bags in the pepper and spices section of Asian grocery stores.

1

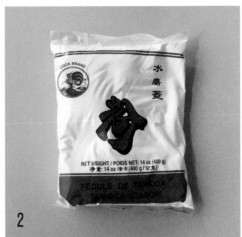

2

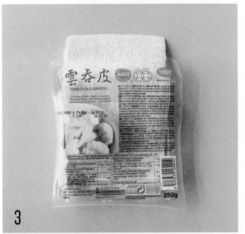

3

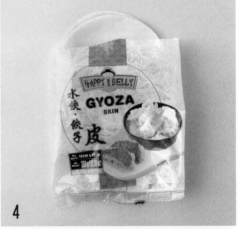

4

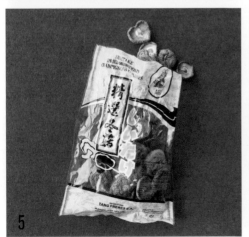

5

6

Shaoxing wine or hua diao jiu / hua tiao chiew: (meaning 'etched flower', a motif on jars of wine). This is a type of alcohol produced by fermenting sticky rice. It has an amber colour and a very sweet flavour, similar to sherry. If you can't find any, you can use saké instead. Used for marinades and for cooking meat.

Kwantung mijiu: Guangzhou rice wine produced by fermenting rice and soybeans. It has an alcoholic strength of 29 per cent, similar to white spirits. It can be substituted with mirin or vodka. It enhances the flavour of prawns and fish but can also be used to balance out sweet dishes such as caramelised pork.

Oyster sauce (in Chinese, 'oyster milk or oil'): A thick, brown sauce with a sweet-and-sour flavour, which gives dishes that famous fifth flavour: 'umami'. Like soy sauce, oyster sauce is a staple of Chinese cooking. The most famous brand is Lee Kum Kee®. In 1888, the Guangzhou-based artisan created the sauce by accident when he left a dish of oysters on the hob, creating a black, richly fragranced stock at the bottom of the pan. Nowadays, oyster sauce is a mixture of oysters, soy, sugar and thickener. Choose a sauce with a high percentage of oysters: this can vary anywhere between 3 per cent and 45 per cent depending on the brand.

Hoisin sauce: Chinese barbecue sauce. Thick and brown with a strong sweet-and-sour flavour. Made by fermenting salted soybeans, sugar, and rice vinegar. Essential for making caramelised pork (char siu, page 18).

It is normally used in marinades for meat (pork and duck), or as a sauce for Peking duck. It comes in different types of packaging: in a plastic bottle, glass jar or a jar. Once opened, it can be kept in the refrigerator for several months.

Black rice vinegar – yonghun laogu: made by fermenting sticky rice and red yeast rice. It has an acidic taste and a low alcohol content. It is mainly used with ginger as a sauce for dumplings (xiaolong bao) or to season Pekinese soup.

Chinkiang black rice vinegar: made with sticky rice, wheat bran and sugar. Sweeter than its cousin and with a fruity flavour, it is perfect in salad dressings. It can also be used as a dip for dumplings or for creating your own sauce mix.

Sichuan pepper: actually a berry. It has a peppery, slightly spicy flavour with a hint of lemon. It produces a slight sensation of numbness on your tongue. Mostly used with beef, pork, and duck. But a little touch on prawns or white fish can create a nice effect. Essential for making spiced chilli oil (page 116).

TIPS
& ADVICE

MATERIALS

STEAMING: to cook steamed dumplings and bao buns, you can use:

• An electric steamer with several steam levels. Make sure the baskets are high enough though, as bao buns expand while cooking.

• Bamboo baskets, which come in different sizes to fit your saucepan. The downside of steam baskets is that they become warped over time and are not completely watertight. The steam escapes from the sides and cooking takes longer. But they are inexpensive and aesthetically pleasing.

• Stainless-steel baskets. While very practical and hard-wearing, they are a little on the small side for bao buns.

They will only hold two or three buns per basket. Perfect for dumplings though.

• If you have a large family and a gas stove, I recommend investing in a Chinese steamer. They come in all sizes up to a diameter of 40 cm (16 in), and you can stack three or four baskets on top of each other. Even if the label says 'stainless steel', these pans cannot be used on an induction hob.

You will find them in large Asian supermarkets or in Chinese stores that sell catering and takeaway equipment.

ROLLER: classic rolling pins are not suitable for the disc shape of dumplings and bao buns. I strongly recommend investing in a small, inexpensive roller, which

you can get either from Chinese catering stores or online. They have no handles. Or you could also use a small bottle or cylindrical tube made from any type of wood. Ideally, the roller should be no longer than 22–28 cm (8½–11 in) and between 2–2.5 cm (¾–1 in) in diameter.

FRYING PAN AND LID: to pan-cook dumplings, you will need a non-stick pan with a suitable lid or a perfectly seasoned pan. Once the water has evaporated, toast the bottom of the dumplings, then lift them out carefully to make sure they don't break.

PLANNING

• Choose a quiet day for making dumplings. Don't try and make them an hour before it's time to serve them. It is best to make them in the morning and leave them in the freezer until you're ready to dish up.

• Ask someone to help you. One person can knead the dough while the other does the folding.

• At the start, use a cutter to make perfectly round discs. This will make the folding stage easier.

Over time, as you gradually get more adept at rolling out the dough, you will find you can also fold them with an imperfect disc.

• Place each dumpling on a tray or a large dish lined with baking parchment. Check that the dish fits into your freezer. If it is a warm day, or if you are making fragile dumplings (i.e., soup dumplings), put the dish into the freezer.

• To make an assortment of dumplings, freeze half your dumplings each time you make some and use a different recipe for the next batch.

• When steam-cooking, line the basket with non-stick baking parchment or use salad leaves (without the veins) to create a flat surface. Never put the dumplings directly into the basket; you won't be able to get them out without breaking them.

TIPS & ADVICE

Here are some practical tips to make sure your bao bun and dim sum recipes go perfectly to plan each time.

BAO BUNS

FILLING: always prepare your filling one day in advance, or even the day before that. It will absorb the flavours better and, most importantly, this will enable you to shape the filling into balls and to make sure your garnish is nice and cold, which will help when it comes to folding your bao buns.

SQUARES OF NON-STICK BAKING PARCHMENT: cut them out in advance or while the dough is rising.

KNEADING: don't overlook the kneading stage. Once you have combined all the ingredients, knead the dough with the palm of your hand for a good five minutes on the work surface. Use a timer to make sure you stick to the timings.

PROOFING: for optimal results, it is essential that you leave your dough to rise for long enough. If your dough has not doubled in size, leave it longer. The longer the dough rests, the more the flavours will develop and the lighter it will be.

FOLDING: if you find the folding stage tedious, fold the dough over the filling like a purse and pinch firmly on the centre to seal it and close the bun.

COOKING: once you have made your bao buns, arrange them in the steamer baskets, well spaced apart, so you don't have to move them again once they have risen. Don't forget that they will rise even more while cooking. Once they are cooked, take them out of the basket straight away to stop any residual water from the steam from wetting the dough.

STORAGE: once they are cooked, bao buns can be stored in the refrigerator for a week. To reheat, simply steam them for 8–10 minutes. Cover with cling film (plastic wrap) or store in an airtight container. Bao buns are generally enjoyed as a snack but they can be made into a meal by serving one or two buns per person with some side dishes.

DIM SUM

FILLING: as with bao buns, prepare your filling a day or two in advance. It will taste all the better for it, and you will be less stressed when it comes to folding your dumplings.

Wheat flour dough: as with bao buns, the kneading stage is very important. The dough will seem dry at first, but as you knead it, it will gradually soak up what might seem like a surplus of flour. Make all your discs of dough before you begin folding. Dust the work surface with flour between each disc to stop them from sticking to one another.

Starch pastry: wrap in cling film (plastic wrap) to stop it from drying out and becoming brittle, and shape your dumplings as soon as you have rolled out the dough.

FOLDING: if you are a complete beginner, take this stage one step at a time:
• Buy a packet of gyoza pastry wrappers. Try a simple fold, like a half-moon shape.
• Then move on to the next step by trying out a Peking dumpling fold.
• Next, make the pastry yourself using wheat flour.
• And lastly, make starch pastry with either a half-moon fold (fun guo, page 50) or a har gao fold (page 136).

PAN-FRYING: You can judge the amount of water needed for pan-frying dumplings simply by looking at it. The water should reach up to about a third of the height of the dumplings. If you are unsure, I recommend adding less water. Once all the water has evaporated, you can gauge whether you have enough by how well cooked the dough is; it should be nice and soft. If you add too much water at the start, it will be too late to rectify the situation and the dumplings will turn mushy.

STORAGE: dumplings can be stored in the refrigerator for a month. You don't need to defrost them; simply increase the cooking time by about 5 minutes. For pan-fried dumplings, add a little more water.

Bao ou *bao zi*, means 'little bag', 'bag', or 'envelope' in Chinese

Originating from northern China, a 'bao' is a stuffed bun made with wheat flour, water and yeast. It is usually steamed. There are lots of different types of bao buns: they come in various sizes, have different fillings and are cooked in different ways (steamed, oven-cooked, pan-fried) depending on the region.
Bao buns sold at street food stalls are on the larger side and are made with a simple pork, cauliflower or garlic chive filling. In Guangzhhou and in the south, they are smaller and have a sweet flavour, like chair siu bao (caramelised pork). You will also find baked bao and sweet bao buns in the South. In Shanghai, restaurants sell more sophisticated types of bao buns.

The Xia Long Bao, encased in a wrapping as thin as a ravioli sheet, contains a soup filling which you need to eat with a spoon to avoid burning yourself. In Taiwan, gua bao buns come in the form of little sandwiches which are filled once cooked.

Choose the bao that most tickles your taste buds!

HOMEMADE
BAO

MAMA'S
MINCED PORK & BABY VEGETABLE BAO BUNS
媽媽的包

Makes **12 bao buns**
Soaking **40 mins**
Preparation **1 hr 30 mins**
Rising **2 hrs**
Cooking **15 mins**

Filling
10 g (½ oz) dried shiitake
   mushrooms
10 g (½ oz) dried wood ear
   mushrooms
30 g (1 oz) onion
50 g (2 oz) tinned chestnuts
   (optional)
60 g (2 oz) carrot
1 tbsp vegetable oil
1 garlic clove, pressed
3 tbsp soy sauce
60 ml (2 fl oz) water
½ bunch of coriander
500 g (1 lb oz) minced
   (ground) pork breast
1 heaped tbsp potato starch
1 egg
3 tbsp soy sauce
15 g (½ oz) sugar (1 tbsp)
1 tbsp sesame oil
1 level tsp salt
black pepper

Extra-soft pastry
Mixture 1
265 g (9½ oz) strong white
   bread flour, sifted, plus
   extra for dusting
8 g (¼ oz/2 tsp)) instant dried
   yeast
225 ml (8 fl oz) warm water
   (35°C/95°F)
Mixture 2
130 g (4½ oz) strong white
   bread flour, sifted
16.5 g (½ oz) baking powder
75 g (2½ oz) brown sugar
40 g (1½ oz) melted butter

Filling

Soak the shiitake and wood ear mushrooms in a large pot of hot water for 40 minutes.

Chop the onion and finely dice the chestnuts and carrot. Once rehydrated, strain the mushrooms.

Roughly chop the wood ear mushrooms and finely dice the shiitake mushrooms. Heat the vegetable oil in a small pan.

Gently fry the garlic and shiitake mushrooms for 2 minutes then add 1 tablespoon of soy sauce and the water. Continue cooking for 5 minutes until the water has evaporated. Leave to cool.

Chop the coriander (leaves and stems). Combine all the filling ingredients and season generously with pepper. You can heat a bit of the filling in the microwave for 15 seconds to check the seasoning: adjust if necessary. Weigh the filling and divide into 12 balls. Set aside in the refrigerator. The filling can be made the night before.

Extra-soft pastry

Preheat the oven to its lowest setting. Combine the flour and yeast. Pour in the warm water and whisk. Cover with a dish towel and leave to stand for 1 hour in the switched-off oven. The dough should form bubbles and double in volume. Cut out 12 squares of baking parchment measuring 6–7 cm (2½–2¾ in) on each side.

Combine the flour, baking powder and sugar from mixture 2.

Pour into mixture 1 a little at a time, mixing by hand. Add the cold melted butter and continue mixing. When the dough is nice and even, pour it out onto a lightly floured work surface and knead with the palm of your hand until it no longer sticks to your hands. Add more flour if needed. Weigh the dough. Roll out into a log and divide into 12 balls.

Folding & cooking

Dust the work surface with flour and roll out each ball of dough, making sure the centre is thicker than the edges. Make your bao buns (page 132). Lay each bun on a square of baking parchment – they will expand while cooking. Place the buns in the steamer baskets, spaced apart, cover with a dish towel and leave to rise for 1 hour.

Pour plenty of water into a steamer. When the water comes to the boil, turn down the heat slightly and add the baskets. Cook for 15 minutes. Remove the cooked buns with a spatula and repeat the same steps for the remaining buns. Enjoy hot.

Storage
These buns can be kept in the refrigerator for up to 5 days. To reheat, steam for 10 minutes.

PORK WITH
CHINESE BARBECUE SAUCE (CHAR SIU BAO)
叉燒包

Makes **10 bao buns**
Preparation **1 hr**
Chilling **1 night**
Proofing **2 hrs**
Cooking **15 mins**

Filling
500 g (1 lb 2 oz) pork
   shoulder
15 g (½ oz/1 tbsp) brown
   sugar
2 tbsp soy sauce
1 very large tbsp oyster
   sauce
2 tbsp hoisin sauce
20 ml (¾ fl oz/4 tsp) rice wine
60 ml (2 fl oz) water
15 g (½ oz/2 tbsp) Maïzena®
black pepper

Classic pastry
300 g (10½ oz) strong white
   bread flour, sifted, plus
   extra for dusting
8 g (¼ oz/2 tsp) instant dried
   baker's yeast
40 g (1½ oz) sugar
1 tsp bicarbonate of soda
   (baking soda) (optional)
1 heaped tsp salt
165 ml (5½ fl oz) water
1½ tbsp vegetable oil

Filling

Make the filling the day before. Cut the pork shoulder into 1 cm (½ in) cubes. In a saucepan, combine the brown sugar, sauces, rice wine and water.

Bring to the boil. Add the meat, season with pepper and cook for 10 minutes, stirring occasionally. Dilute the Maïzena® with a bit of water. Pour into a pan, stirring constantly, and boil for a few minutes until thickened. Leave to cool completely and set aside in the refrigerator until the next day.

Classic pastry

Preheat the oven to its lowest setting. In a container, mix together all the pastry ingredients, except the warm water and oil. Make a well in the centre and pour in the oil, then add the warm water and mix by hand. When the dough begins to blend together, pour it out onto a work surface and knead until nice and smooth; the kneading should take a good 5 minutes. The dough should not stick to your hands. Shape into a ball, cover with a clean dish towel and leave to rise for 1 hour in the switched-off oven or in a warm place. The dough should double in size.

Cut out 10 squares of baking paper measuring 6–7 cm (2½–2¾ in) on each side.

Folding & cooking

Weigh the dough and divide into 10 balls. Dust the work surface with flour and roll out each ball of dough, making sure the centre is thicker than the edges. Spoon over 1 large tablespoon of filling (60 g/2 oz) and fold (page 132). Place each bao bun on a square of baking paper. Place the buns in steamer baskets, spaced apart, cover with a dish towel and leave to rise for 1 hour. Bring some water to the boil in a saucepan. Reduce the heat slightly, add the steamer baskets and cook for 15 minutes. Enjoy your bao buns when they have cooled down slightly.

DUCK,
MUSHROOM & FIVE-SPICE
五香鴨肉包

Makes **8 bao buns**
Preparation **1 hr 30 mins**
Proofing **2 hrs**
Cooking **15 mins**

Filling
2 duck leg confits, tinned
1 large onion
3 large garlic cloves
500 g (1 lb 2 oz) button
    mushrooms
2 large tbsp hoisin sauce
1 level tsp Chinese five-spice
    powder
½ tsp Sichuan pepper
½ small bunch of flat-leaf
    parsley
½ bunch of chives
½ small bunch of dill
salt and black pepper

Classic pastry
300 g (10½ oz) strong white
    bread flour, sifted, plus
    extra for dusting
8 g (¼ oz/2 tsp) instant dried
    yeast
40 g (1½ oz) sugar
1 tsp bicarbonate of soda
    (baking soda) (optional)
1 heaped tsp salt
165 ml (5½ fl oz) warm water
1½ tbsp vegetable oil
3 tbsp chopped herbs (such
    as flat-leaf parsley, dill,
    chives)

Tip
Use any remaining filling with
stir-fried noodles or to make
dumplings with wonton pastry
wrappers.

Filling

Wash the mushrooms, cut the biggest ones in half then slice. Chop
the onion and press the garlic cloves. Chop the herbs and set aside
3 tablespoons for the pastry.

Remove the skin from the duck legs and pull the skin apart roughly with
a fork. The biggest pieces of skin will come apart while cooking. Reserve
3 tablespoons duck fat.

Grind the Sichuan pepper in a mortar or with a rolling pin.

Heat the duck fat in a pan. Sauté the onion for 2 minutes then add the
mushrooms. Season with salt and pepper. Continue cooking until the
mushrooms start to brown. Add the duck skin, garlic, hoisin sauce, five-
spice powder and Sichuan pepper. Continue cooking for 5 minutes, stirring
from time to time. Taste and adjust the seasoning if necessary. Remove
from the heat and add the herbs. Set aside to cool completely. The filling
can be made the day beforehand.

Classic pastry

Preheat the oven to its lowest setting. Mix together all the pastry
ingredients, except the warm water and oil, in a container. Make a well in
the centre, pour in the oil, then add the warm water and mix by hand. When
the dough starts to come together, pour it out onto a work surface
and knead until it is nice and smooth; the kneading should take a good
5 minutes. The dough should not stick to your hands. Shape into a ball,
cover with a clean dish towel and leave to rise for 1 hour in the switched-off
oven or warm place. The dough should double in size. Cut out 8 squares of
baking parchment measuring 6–7 cm (2½–2¾ in) on each side.

Folding & cooking

Make eight balls of filling weighing 70 g (2½ oz) each. Weigh the dough and
divide into eight balls. Dust the work surface with flour and roll out each ball
of dough, making sure the centre is thicker than the edges.

Take one ball of filling and start folding (page 132).

Place each bun on a square of baking parchment. Lay the buns in the
steamer baskets, spaced apart, cover with a dish towel and leave to rise
for 1 hour.

Bring some water to the boil in a saucepan. Reduce the heat slightly, add
the baskets and cook for 15 minutes. Enjoy your bao buns as soon as they
have cooled down slightly.

AUBERGINE
& MINCED PORK (HONGSHAO STYLE)
紅燒茄子豬肉包

Makes **8 bao buns**
Preparation **1 hr 30 mins**
Resting **30 mins**
Proofing **2 hrs**
Cooking **15 mins**

Filling
300 g (10½ oz) aubergine
  (eggplant)
3 garlic cloves
20 g (¾ oz) fresh ginger root
3 Asian chives, scallions or
  spring onions
3 tbsp vegetable oil
150 g (5 oz) minced (ground)
  pork
8 g (¼ oz/2 tsp) sugar
3 tbsp soy sauce
60 ml (2 fl oz) water
salt and black pepper

Classic beetroot pastry
300 g (10½ oz) strong white
  bread flour, sifted, plus
  extra for dusting
8 g (¼ oz/2 tsp) instant dried
  yeast
40 g (1½ oz) sugar
1 tsp bicarbonate of soda
  (baking soda) (optional)
1 heaped tsp salt
125 ml (4 fl oz) water
40 ml (1⅓ fl oz/2⅔ tbsp)
  beetroot (beet) juice
1½ tbsp vegetable oil

Note
While cooking, the beetroot
(beet) will change from pink
to yellowy orange.

Filling
Wash and dice the aubergines. Season with salt, mix and leave to drain in
a colander for 30 minutes. Chop the garlic, thinly slice the ginger then dice.
Chop the Asian chives.

Dry the aubergines with a dish towel or paper towel.

Heat the oil in a large frying pan (skillet). Brown the aubergines on all sides
then remove from the pan. In the same pan, brown the garlic and ginger.
Add a bit of oil if needed. When the vegetables begin to brown, add the
minced pork and stir to separate the clumps of meat. Add the sugar and
soy sauce.

Season with plenty of pepper. Return the aubergines to the pan and add
the water. Reduce the heat and cook for 10 minutes. The water should
evaporate and the aubergines should be soft. Prick with the end of a knife
to check it is cooked. Remove from the heat and add the chopped Asian
chives/spring onions.

Set aside to cool completely. You can make the filling the day before.

Classic beetroot pastry
Preheat the oven to its lowest setting. Combine the water and beetroot
juice. In a large bowl, combine all the pastry ingredients, except the oil
and beetroot water. Make a well in the centre and pour in the oil, then
add the beetroot water and stir by hand. When the dough starts to blend
together, pour it out onto a work surface and knead until it is nice and
smooth; the kneading should take a good 5 minutes. The dough should not
stick to your hands. Shape into a ball, cover with a clean dish towel and
leave to rise for 1 hour in the switched-off oven or warm place. The dough
should double in volume. Cut out 8 squares of baking parchment measuring
6–7 cm (2½–2¾ in) on each side.

Folding & cooking
Weigh the dough and divide into eight balls. Dust the work surface with
flour and roll out each ball of dough, making sure the centre is thicker
than the edges. Take two spoonfuls of filling (70 g/2½ oz) and start folding
(page 132). Place each bao bun on a square of baking parchment.

Arrange the bao buns in the steamer baskets, spaced apart, cover
with a dish towel and leave to rise for 1 hour. Bring some water to the
boil in a saucepan. Reduce the heat slightly, add the baskets and cook for
15 minutes. Enjoy your bao buns as soon as they have cooled down slightly.

Tip
You can substitute the 60 ml (2 oz) water for the filling with Shaoxing wine.

SPICED PULLED
PORK
花椒手撕豬肉包

Makes **12 bao buns**
Preparation 1 hr 15 mins
Chilling **1 night**
Proofing **2 hrs**
Cooking **2 hr 30 mins**
+ 15 mins

Filling

1 kg (2 lb 4 oz) pork shoulder
1 large onion, quartered
1 small head of garlic, halved
   horizontally
80 g (3 oz) fresh ginger root,
   cut into strips
80 ml (3 fl oz) soy sauce
40 g (1½ oz) brown sugar
   or semolina
1 cinnamon stick
2 star anise
4 bay leaves
1 bunch of coriander
   (cilantro)
1 tbsp coarse Sichuan pepper
   or black pepper
6 spring onions (scallions)

Extra-soft pastry
Mixture 1
265 g (9½ oz) strong white
   bread flour, sifted, plus
   extra for dusting
8 g (¼ oz/2 tsp) instant dried
   yeast
225 ml (8 fl oz) warm water
   (35°C/95°F)
Mixture 2
130 g (4½ oz) strong white
   bread flour, sifted
16.5 g (½ oz) baking powder
75 g (2½ oz) brown sugar
40 g (1½ oz) melted butter

Filling

The day before, slow-cook the pork. Preheat the oven to 180°C (350°F/ gas mark 4). In a casserole dish (Dutch oven), combine all the filling ingredients, except for the spring onions. Cover with water, bring to the boil and bake in the oven for 2½ hours, turning the meat occasionally.

When the meat is cooked, lay it out on a dish. Strain the sauce and reduce by half until it becomes syrupy. Shred the meat with a fork. Add the sauce a little at a time, tasting to check. Add the chopped spring onion, stir and chill overnight.

Extra-soft pastry

Preheat the oven to its lowest setting. Mix together the flour and yeast in a large bowl. Whisk in the warm water. Cover with a clean dish towel and set aside in the switched-off oven for 1 hour. The dough should form bubbles and double in size.

Cut out squares of baking parchment measuring 6–7 cm (2½–2¾ in) on each side.

Mix together the flour, baking powder, and sugar from mixture 2. Pour into mixture 1 a little at a time, stirring by hand. Add the cold melted butter and continue to mix. When the dough is nice and even, pour it out onto a lightly floured work surface and knead with the palm of your hand until it no longer sticks to your hands. Add more flour if needed.

Folding & cooking

Weigh the filling and divide into 12 balls. Weigh the dough. Roll it out into a log and divide into 12 balls.

Dust the work surface with flour and roll out each ball of dough, making sure the centre is thicker than the edges. Drop a ball of filling onto the centre and start making your bao buns (page 132). Place each bun on a square of baking parchment. Arrange them in the steamer baskets, spaced apart, cover with a dish towel and leave to rise for 1 hour. Bring some water to the boil in a saucepan. Reduce the heat slightly, add the baskets and cook for 15 minutes. Enjoy your bao buns as soon as they have cooled down.

CHICKEN, LEMONGRASS & PEANUTS

泰式花生雞肉包

Makes **8 bao buns**
Preparation **1 hr 15 mins**
Proofing **2 hrs**
Cooking **15 mins**

Filling

500 g (1 lb 2 oz) boneless
   chicken thighs
2 garlic cloves
20 g (¾ oz) fresh ginger root
2 sticks of lemongrass
1 heaped tbsp brown sugar
2 tbsp nuoc-mâm
   (Vietnamese dipping sauce)
½ bunch of coriander
   (cilantro) (optional)
40 g (1½ oz) roasted and
   salted peanuts
½ tsp salt
black pepper

Traditional chilli pastry

300 g (10½ oz) strong white
   bread flour, sifted, plus
   extra for dusting
8 g (¼ oz/2 tsp) instant dried
   baker's yeast
40 g (1½ oz) sugar
1 tsp bicarbonate of soda
   (baking soda) (optional)
1 heaped tsp salt
165 ml (5½ fl oz) warm water
1 heaped tbsp Korean chilli
   powder or paprika
1½ tbsp vegetable oil

Filling

Cut the chicken into strips. Press the garlic and grate the ginger. Remove the hard parts from the lemongrass and finely slice the soft stalks. Chop the coriander. Combine these ingredients with the chicken, then add the sugar, salt and nuoc-mâm. Season with pepper and leave to marinate while you make the pastry. The filling can be made the day before.

Classic chilli pastry

Preheat the oven to its lowest setting. Combine all the pastry ingredients, except the oil and warm water, in a large bowl. Make a well in the centre, pour in the oil, then add the warm water and mix by hand. When the dough starts to blend together, pour it out onto a work surface and knead until it is nice and smooth; the kneading should take a good 5 minutes. The dough should not stick to your hands. Shape into a ball, cover with a clean dish towel and leave to rise for 1 hour in a switched-off oven or warm place. The dough should double in size.

Cut out 8 squares of baking parchment measuring 6–7 cm (2½–2¾ in) on each side. Roughly chop the peanuts.

Folding & cooking

Weigh the filling and divide into eight balls. Drop 1 small spoonful of chopped peanuts onto each ball. Press down with your hand so they stick.

Weigh the dough and divide it into eight balls. Dust the work surface with flour and roll out each ball of dough, making sure the centre is thicker than the edges. Add the ball of filling and start folding (page 132). Place each bao bun on a square of baking parchment. Arrange the buns in the steamer baskets, spaced apart, cover with a dish towel and leave to rise for 1 hour.

Bring some water to the boil in a saucepan. Reduce the heat slightly, add the steamer baskets and cook for 15 minutes. Enjoy your bao buns as soon as they have cooled down. You can serve these buns with coconut, miso & lime sauce (page 118).

VEGETABLE
CURRY BAO BUNS
咖喱蔬菜包

Makes 8 bao buns
Preparation **1 hr 15 mins**
Proofing **2 hrs**
Cooking **15 mins**

Vegetable curry
1 onion
1 garlic clove
10 g (¼ oz) fresh ginger root
300 g (10½ oz) butternut
  squash
125 g (4 oz) spinach
30 g (1 oz/2 tbsp) red lentils
200 ml (7 fl oz) coconut milk
50 ml (1¾ fl oz/3 tbsp) water

Classic curry pastry
300 g (10½ oz) strong white
  bread flour, sifted, plus
  extra for dusting
8 g (¼ oz/2 tsp) dried baker's
  yeast
40 g (1½ oz) sugar
1 tsp bicarbonate of soda
  (baking soda) (optional)
1 heaped tsp salt
165 g (5½ fl oz) water
1 heaped tbsp Madras curry
  powder
1.5 tbsp vegetable oil

Tip
To make the shaping easier,
wrap 70 g (2½ oz) curry
in cling film (plastic wrap).
Seal the cling film and roll to
make a ball. Freeze the balls
of filling.

Filling

Chop the onion, press the garlic, and grate the ginger. Cut the squash into 6–8 mm (¼–⁵⁄₁₆ in) cubes. Roughly chop the spinach.

In a saucepan, combine all the curry ingredients except for the spinach. Season with salt and add 50 ml (1.7 fl oz) water. Cover and cook over a very low heat for 20 minutes. Stir regularly to stop the bottom from sticking. Taste to see if it is cooked and to check the seasoning.

The curry should be thick, like a purée. Add a tiny bit of water and continue cooking if necessary. Add the spinach, stir, and stop cooking. Set aside to cool completely. It is best to make the curry the day before, so it is set in time for folding.

Classic curry pastry

Preheat the oven to its lowest setting. In a large bowl, combine all the pastry ingredients, except the oil and water. Make a well in the centre, pour in the oil, then add the water and stir by hand.

Stir by hand. When the dough starts to blend together, pour it out onto a work surface and knead until it is nice and smooth; the kneading should take a good 5 minutes. The dough should not stick to your hands. Make a ball, cover with a clean dish towel and leave to rise for 1 hour in a switched-off oven or warm place. The dough should double in size.

Cut out 8 squares of baking parchment measuring 6–7 cm (2½–2¾ in) on each side.

Folding & cooking

Weigh the dough and divide into eight balls. Dust the work surface with flour and roll out each ball of dough, making sure the centre is thicker than the edges. Add two spoonfuls of filling and start folding (page 132). Place each bao bun on a square of baking parchment. Add the buns to the steamer baskets, spaced apart, and cook for 15 minutes. Enjoy your bao buns as soon as they have cooled.

TOFU
BOK CHOY & SHIITAKE
什錦蔬菜包

Makes **8 bao buns**
Soaking **2 hrs**
Preparation **1 hr 20 mins**
Proofing **2 hrs**
Cooking **15 mins**

Filling

1 onion, chopped
6 dried shiitake mushrooms
15 g (½ oz) dried wood ear
   mushrooms
3 tbsp vegetable oil
150 g (5 oz) tofu
100 ml (3½ fl oz) Shaoxing
   wine
2 tbsp oyster sauce
1 tbsp hoisin sauce
2 tbsp soy sauce
1 tsp sugar
450 g (1 lb) bok choy, thinly
   sliced
2 large garlic cloves, pressed
black pepper

Classic green pastry

100 g (3½ oz) spinach
180 ml (6 fl oz) water
300 g (10½ oz) strong white
   bread flour, sifted, plus
   extra for dusting
8 g (¼ oz/2 tsp) instant dried
   yeast
40 g (1½ oz) sugar
½ tsp bicarbonate of soda
   (baking soda) (optional)
1 heaped tsp salt
1½ tbsp vegetable oil

Tip

To make the green water for
the pastry, you can use fresh
spinach stems or frozen
spinach.

Filling

Rehydrate the onion in a large bowl of water, ideally the day before. Alternatively, soak them in boiling water for at least 2 hours. Strain, chop the shiitake and roughly chop the wood ear mushrooms. Heat the oil in a frying pan (skillet). Brown the onion, shiitake and tofu for 5 minutes.

Add the wine, oyster sauce, hoisin sauce, soy sauce, and sugar. Season with pepper and reduce until nearly evaporated. Add the bok choy, wood ear mushrooms and garlic. Brown for 3 minutes.

Taste and adjust the seasoning if necessary. Leave to cool completely.

Classic green pastry

Preheat the oven to its lowest setting.

Mix the spinach with the 180 ml (6 fl oz) water. Strain and weigh out 165 g (5½ fl oz) water.

You can add 1 tablespoon of spinach pulp to the filtered water to enhance the flavour.

Combine all the pastry ingredients, except the oil and green water, in a large bowl. Make a well in the centre, pour in the oil, then add the green water and mix by hand. When the dough starts to blend together, pour it out onto the work surface and knead until it is nice and smooth; the kneading will take a good 5 minutes. The dough should not stick to your hands. Shape into a ball, cover with a clean dish towel and leave to rise for 1 hour in a switched off oven or warm place. The dough should double in volume.

Cut out 8 squares of baking paper measuring 6–7 cm (2½–2¾ in) on each side.

Folding & cooking

Weigh the dough and divide into eight balls. Dust the work surface with flour and roll out each ball of dough, making sure that the centre is thicker than the edges. Add two spoonfuls of filling and start folding (page 132). Use your left thumb to help push the filling inside the dough. Place each bao bun on a square of baking parchment. Add the buns to the steamer baskets, spaced apart, cover with a dish towel and leave to rise for 1 hour. Bring some water to the boil in a saucepan. Reduce the heat slightly, add the baskets and cook for 15 minutes.

Enjoy your buns as soon as they have cooled.

TWISTED BAO BUNS
WITH SPRING ONION (HUA JUAN)
香蔥花捲

Makes **8 twisted bao buns**
Preparation **45 mins**
Proofing **1 hr 40 mins**
Cooking **12–15 mins**

Classic pastry

300 g (10½ oz) strong white
    bread flour, sifted, plus
    extra for dusting
8 g (¼ oz/2 tsp) instant dried
    yeast
40 g (1½ oz) sugar
½ tsp bicarbonate of soda
    (baking soda) (optional)
1 heaped tsp salt
1½ tbsp vegetable oil
165 ml (5½ fl oz) water

Garnish

4 spring onions (scallions)
    or the green part of a fresh
    onion
3 tbsp vegetable oil or chilli
    oil (page 116)
1 level tsp Chinese
    five-spice powder
salt and black pepper

Classic pastry

Preheat the oven to its lowest setting. Preheat the oven to its lowest setting. Combine all the pastry ingredients, except the oil and water, in a large bowl. Make a well in the centre, pour in the oil, then add the water and mix by hand. When the dough starts to blend together, pour it out onto the work surface and knead until it is nice and smooth; the kneading should take a good 5 minutes. The dough should not stick to your hands. Shape into a ball, cover with a clean dish towel and leave to rise in the switched-off oven or in a warm place for 1 hour. The dough should double in size.

Folding & cooking

Finely chop the spring onions. Cut out 8 squares of baking parchment measuring 6–7 cm (2½–2¾ in) on each side.

Dust the work surface and roll out the dough into a 40 x 30 cm (16 x 12 in) rectangle. Brush the dough with oil using a pastry brush. Dust with salt pepper and five-spice powder. Sprinkle over the chopped spring onions then fold and cut out your twisted bao buns (page 134). Place each bun on a square of baking parchment. Arrange the twisted bao buns in the steamer baskets, spaced apart, cover with a dish towel and leave to rise for 40 minutes.

Bring some water to the boil in a saucepan. Reduce the heat slightly, add the baskets and cook for 12–15 minutes. Enjoy when they have cooled down slightly, either on their own or alongside other side dishes or salads.

TWO-COLOURED BAO BUNS
WITH COPPA & SUNDRIED TOMATOES
番茄火腿雙色花卷

Makes **8 twisted bao buns**
Preparation **45 mins**
Proofing **1 hr 40 mins**
Cooking **12–15 mins**

Classic pastry
300 g (10½ oz) strong white
 bread flour, sifted, plus
 extra for dusting
8 g (¼ oz/2 tsp) instant dried
 yeast
40 g (1½ oz) sugar
½ tsp bicarbonate of soda
 (baking soda) (optional)
1 heaped tsp salt
1½ tbsp vegetable oil
165 ml (5½ fl oz) water

Classic green pastry
70 g (2½ oz) spinach
150 ml (5 fl oz) hot water
200 g (7 oz) strong white
 bread flour, sifted, plus
 extra for dusting
½ tsp instant dried yeast
25 g (1 oz/2 tbsp) sugar
½ tsp bicarbonate of soda
 (baking soda) (optional)
½ tsp salt
1 tbsp vegetable oil

Garnish
3 slices of coppa
30 g (1 oz) sundried tomatoes
2 tbsp olive oil
2 spring onions (scallions)
salt and freshly ground black
 pepper

Vegan version
Replace the coppa with black
olives.

Classic pastry

Preheat the oven to its lowest setting. Combine all the white pastry ingredients, except the oil and warm water, in a large bowl. Make a well in the centre, pour in the oil, then add the warm water and mix by hand. When the dough starts to blend, pour it out onto the work surface and knead until it is nice and smooth; the kneading should take a good 5 minutes. The dough should not stick to your hands. Shape it into a ball, cover with a clean dish towel and leave to rise for 1 hour in the switched-off oven or in a warm place. The dough should double in size.

Classic green pastry

Make green pastry by combining the spinach with the hot water.

Strain the green juice and weigh out 110 g (3.5 oz). Follow the same instructions as for the white pastry then leave to rise for 1 hour in a warm place.

Folding & cooking

Finely slice the coppa, sundried tomatoes and spring onions. Cut out 12 squares of baking parchment measuring 6 cm (2½ in) on each side.

Dust the work surface with flour and roll out the white dough into a 35 x 22 cm (14 x 8½ in) rectangle (page 150). Brush the dough with olive oil using a pastry brush. Season with salt and pepper and scatter over the chopped spring onions. Fold the dough in three and cut out 12 strips. Set aside.

Roll out the green dough to the same size. Brush with oil, season very lightly then garnish with coppa and tomatoes. Fold the dough in three, cut out 12 strips and start shaping your twisted bao buns by placing two strips of each colour on top of one another (page 134). Place each bun on a square of baking paper. Place the buns in the steamer baskets, spaced apart, cover with a dish towel and leave to rise for 40 minutes. Bring some water to the boil in a saucepan. Turn down the heat slightly, add the baskets and cook for 12–15 minutes.

GUA BAO BUNS
WITH BRAISED PORK BELLY
滷肉刈包

Makes 12 gua bao buns
Preparation **1 hour**
Proofing **2 hrs**
Cooking **2 hrs 30 mins
+ 12 mins**

Braised pork belly
800 g (1 lb 12 oz) pork belly,
 rind included
80 g (3 oz) fresh ginger root
80 g (3 oz) sugar
½ head of garlic
2 shallots
100 ml (3½ fl oz) soy sauce
50 ml (1¾ fl oz/3 tbsp)
 Shaoxing wine
1 bunch of coriander
 (cilantro) (stalks only)
black pepper

Classic pastry
300 g (10½ oz) strong white
 bread flour, sifted, plus
 extra for dusting
8 g (¼ oz/2 tsp) instant dried
 yeast
40 g (1½ oz) sugar
1 tsp bicarbonate of soda
 (baking soda) (optional)
1 heaped tsp salt
1½ tbsp vegetable oil
165 ml (5½ fl oz) water

Garnish
100 g (3½ oz) roasted
 and salted peanuts
1 cucumber
1 bunch of coriander
 (cilantro) (leaves only)

Planning
Prepare the meat and buns
up to 3 days in advance. To
reheat the buns, steam
for 5 minutes.

Braised pork belly

Chop the shallots. Wash the ginger and slice into strips, with the skin still on. Break off the garlic cloves, place on a cutting board and crush with the flat part of a knife. Pick the leaves off the coriander and reserve them for the garnish. Keep the stalks. Cut the belly into slices (8 cm (3¼ in) long and 1.8 cm/¾ in thick).

Pour the sugar into a casserole dish (Dutch oven) and caramelise. Deglaze the pan with the soy sauce and Shaoxing wine. Add the shallots, garlic, ginger and meat. Stir, cover with water and bring to the boil. Remove any scum from the surface then season generously with pepper and add the coriander stalks. Reduce the heat and simmer for 2 hours 30 minutes.

Classic pastry

Preheat the oven to its lowest setting. Mix all the pastry ingredients, except the oil and water, together in a large bowl. Make a well in the centre, pour in the oil, then add the water and mix by hand. When the dough starts to blend together, pour it out onto the work surface and knead until it is nice and smooth; the kneading should take a good 5 minutes. The dough should not stick to your hands. Shape into a ball, cover with a clean dish towel and leave to rise for 1 hour in the switched-off oven or in a warm place. The dough should double in volume. Cut out 24 rectangles of baking parchments measuring 12 x 7 cm (4½ x 2¾ in).

Gua bao buns

Weigh the dough and divide into 12 balls. Dust the work surface with flour and roll each ball out into an oval (10 cm/4 in wide and 14 cm/5½ in long). Fold the dough in two, sliding a rectangle of baking paper into the middle, then lay it on another rectangle of baking parchment. Arrange the buns in the steamer baskets, spaced apart, cover with a dish towel and leave to rise for 1 hour.

Bring some water to the boil in a saucepan. Turn down the heat slightly, add the baskets and cook for 12 minutes.

Garnish

While the dough is rising, pour half the juice from the meat into a saucepan and reduce by half to make a syrupy sauce. Roughly chop the peanuts and finely slice the cucumber. While the gua bao buns are cooking, reheat the meat over a low heat. When the buns are cooked, open them up and garnish with 1 slice of meat and some slivers of cucumber. Spoon over a little of the reduced sauce and add some cucumber leaves and the peanuts.

You can spice them up by adding sriracha sauce (page 119) or chilli oil (page 116).

GUA BAO BUNS
FRIED CHICKEN (KOREAN STYLE)
炸雞刈包

Makes **12 gua bao buns**
Preparation **1 hr 30 mins**
Proofing **2 hrs**
Cooking **15 mins**

Chicken marinade
4 large boneless chicken
    thighs (800 g/1 lb 12 oz
    total) or chicken breasts
3 garlic cloves
15 g (½ oz) fresh ginger root
2 tbsp sweet soy sauce
1 tbsp oyster sauce
black pepper

Classic pastry
300 g (10½ oz) strong white
    bread flour, sifted, plus
    extra for dusting
8 g (¼ oz/2 tsp) instant dried
    yeast
40 g (1½ oz) sugar
1 tsp bicarbonate of soda
    (baking soda) (optional)
1 heaped tsp salt
1½ tbsp vegetable oil
165 ml (5½ fl oz) water

Pickles
¼ red cabbage
1 large carrot
1 tsp salt
100 ml (3½ fl oz) white rice
    vinegar or cider vinegar
2 tbsp brown sugar

Breadcrumb coating
3 eggs
50 g (2 oz) flour
200g (7 oz) panko
1 tbsp Korean chilli powder
1 tsp garlic powder
salt and black pepper
1.5 litres (50 fl oz) cooking oil

Chicken marinade

Chop the chicken into pieces, ideally 8 x 6 cm (3¼ x 2½ in). Otherwise, chop into pieces which are small enough that you can fit two on each bun. Press the garlic, grate the ginger, and combine with the chicken, sauces, and pepper. Leave to marinate in the refrigerator while you prepare everything else.

Classic pastry

Preheat the oven to its lowest setting. Mix all the pastry ingredients, except the oil and water, together in a large bowl. Make a well in the centre, pour in the oil, then add the water and mix by hand. When the dough starts to blend together, pour it out onto a work surface and knead until it Is nice and smooth; the kneading should take a good 5 minutes. The dough should not stick to your hands. Shape it into a ball, cover with a clean dish towel and leave to rise for 1 hour in the switched-off oven or in a warm place. The dough should double in size. Cut out 24 rectangles of baking parchment measuring 12 x 7 cm (4½ x 2¾ in).

Pickles

Finely slice the cabbage using a mandoline. Grate the carrot. Add the salt, sugar and vinegar. Mix well. Set aside in the refrigerator.

Gua bao buns

Weigh the dough and divide into 12 balls. Dust the work surface with flour and roll each ball out into an oval (10 cm/4 in wide and 14 cm/½ in long). Fold the dough in two, sliding a rectangle of baking parchment into the middle, then lay out on another rectangle of parchment. Arrange the buns in the steamer baskets, spaced apart, cover with a dish towel and leave to rise for 1 hour. Bring some water to the boil in a saucepan. Reduce the heat slightly, add the baskets and cook for 12 minutes.

Breadcrumb coating & garnish

Whisk together the eggs and flour, then season. Mix the panko with the garlic and the chilli powder or paprika. Dunk the pieces of chicken in the egg mixture and then in the panko. Set aside on a wire rack.

Heat the oil in a large frying pan (skillet) at 180°C (350°F). Brown the chicken pieces for 2 minutes. Pat dry on some paper towels. Open up the rolls and garnish with the fried chicken and pickles. Enjoy straight away accompanied by some spicy mayo (page 68) or another sauce of your choice. For a veggie version, replace the chicken with large oyster mushrooms.

BAO BUNS
LITTLE SOUP (SHENG JIAN BAO)
生煎包

Makes **16 bao buns**
Preparation **1 hr**
Chilling **1 night**
Proofing **40 mins**
Cooking **15 mins**

Jelly
200 ml (7 fl oz) chicken stock
½ tsp agar-agar

Filling
300 g (10½ oz) minced
  (ground) pork belly
30 g (1 oz) spring onions
  (scallions), chopped
10 g (¼ oz) fresh ginger root,
  grated
50 ml (1¾ fl oz/3 tbsp)
  chicken stock
2 tbsp soy sauce
1 tbsp sesame oil
1 tbsp Shaoxing wine
  (optional)
1 level tsp salt
1 level tsp sugar
black pepper

Pastry
½ tsp instant dried yeast
125 ml (4 fl oz) warm water
  (35°C/95°F)
200 g (7 oz) strong white
  bread flour, sifted, plus
  extra for dusting
½ tsp salt

Cooking & garnish
2 tbsp vegetable oil
1 tsp toasted sesame seeds,
  to taste
green part of 1 spring onion
  or 2 chives

Jelly & filling

The day before, whisk together the stock and agar-agar in a saucepan. Boil for 1 minute then transfer to a small dish or bowl. Leave to set in the refrigerator overnight. Combine all the filling ingredients, stirring until the stock has been absorbed and the mixture turns slightly sticky. Cover with cling film (plastic wrap) (in direct contact with the surface of the mixture) and leave in the refrigerator overnight.

The next day, chop the jelly into small cubes and mix with the filling. Set aside in the refrigerator while you make the pastry.

Pastry

The next day, mix the yeast with the water. Combine the flour and salt in a large bowl. Make a well in the centre, pour the water in a little at a time, stirring constantly, then knead until the dough is nice and smooth. Shape into a ball and place in a lightly greased bowl. Cover with a dish towel and leave to rest for 40 minutes. Roll out the dough into logs then cut into little 20 g (¾ oz) pieces. Cover the pieces with cling film to stop them from drying out. Dust the work surface with flour and roll the pieces of dough out into discs (with a diameter of 10–12 cm/4 x 4½ in). Ideally, the centre should be a little thicker than the edges. Dollop a large teaspoon of filling onto the centre of each disc of dough. Fold like a soup bao (page 148). Close them well by pinching the centre, otherwise the broth will come out while cooking. Turn your sheng jian bao buns over so that the join is at the bottom. If you think you might not have sealed the buns very well, don't turn them over – keep the folds on top. Repeat with the remaining buns.

Cooking

Heat the oil in a large non-stick frying or cast-iron frying pan. Add the sheng jian bao buns, making sure they are spaced apart slightly. Add about 220 ml (7½ fl oz) water: the water should come up to around a third of the height of the buns. Bring to the boil, reduce the heat to medium, and cover with a lid. When the water has almost evaporated, remove the lid. Cook until there is no water left and the sheng jian bao buns are nicely browned underneath.

Remove from the heat and sprinkle with sesame seeds and chopped spring onions (the green part). Serve your bao buns straight away or leave to cool slightly.

How to eat

Place a sheng jian bao bun on a spoon. Bite into a little bit of the pastry, watching out for the hot broth which will ooze out. Enjoy accompanied by some black vinegar sauce (page 118) or chilli oil mixed with a bit of soy sauce.

CHAR SIU BAO
BAKED
爐烤叉燒包

Makes **8 bao buns**
Preparation **1 hr**
Chilling **1 night**
Proofing **2 hrs 40 mins**
Cooking **25 mins**

Filling

500 g (1 lb 2 oz) pork
  shoulder
15 g (½ oz/1 tbsp) brown
  sugar
2 tbsp soy sauce
1 very large tbsp oyster
  sauce
1 tbsp hoisin sauce
20 ml (¾ fl oz/4 tsp) rice wine
60 ml (2 fl oz) water
15 g (½ oz/2 tbsp) Maïzena®
black pepper

Pastry

6 g (about 1 tsp) instant dried
  yeast
100 ml (3½ fl oz) milk
250 g (9 oz) strong white
  bread flour, plus extra for
  dusting
3 g (¾ tsp) salt
20 g (¾ oz/1 heaped tbsp)
  sugar
1 egg
60 g (2 oz) butter

Glaze

1 egg
3 tbsp milk
2 tbsp black and white
  sesame seeds

Tip

To make your buns glisten,
brush with some maple syrup
when they come out the oven.

Filling

Make the filling the day before. Chop the pork shoulder into 1 cm (½ in) cubes. In a saucepan, combine the brown sugar, sauces, rice wine and water. Bring to the boil. Add the meat, season with pepper, and cook for 10 minutes, stirring occasionally. Dilute the Maïzena® with a bit of water. Pour into the saucepan, stirring constantly, and simmer for a few minutes until thickened. Set aside to cool completely then chill overnight.

Pastry

Combine the yeast with the milk in a bowl or jug. Sift the flour into a stand mixer. Add the salt, sugar and egg. Begin kneading using the dough hook. Add the milk and yeast mixture. Run for 10 minutes until the dough forms a ball that comes away from the sides. Add the diced butter. Knead until completely absorbed. The dough should be smooth and stretchy. As it turns, it should resemble a thread. The kneading should take around another 10 minutes. Cover with a dish towel and leave to rise for 1 hour at room temperature. Fold the dough (lift it up and then let it drop back down again), cover and chill for 1 hour.

Folding & cooking

Weigh the dough and divide into eight balls. Dust the work surface with flour and roll out the balls of dough, making sure the centre is thicker than the edges. Add 1 large tablespoon of filling and start folding (page 132). Make sure you seal the buns well, then turn them over and arrange on a wire rack lined with baking parchment. Cover with a dish towel and leave to rise for 40 minutes.

Preheat the oven to 170°C (325°F/gas mark 3). For the glaze, whisk the egg and milk together in a bowl until combined. Glaze the bao buns using a pastry brush and sprinkle with sesame seeds. Bake in the oven for 25 minutes. Enjoy your bao buns as soon as they have cooled.

BAKED CHICKEN
AND CANDIED LEMON BAO BUNS
爐烤香檸雞肉包

Makes **8 bao buns**
Preparation **1 hr 20 mins**
Proofing **2 hrs 40 mins**
Cooking **25 mins**

Filling

500 g (1 lb 2 oz) boneless
  chicken thighs
1 large carrot
1 large onion
2 garlic cloves
60 g (2 oz) candied lemon
1 small bunch of coriander
  (cilantro)
2 tbsp olive oil
3 tbsp sweet soy sauce
1 heaped tsp turmeric
1 level tsp ground ginger
salt and black pepper

Pastry

6 g (about 1 tsp) instant dried
  yeast
100 ml (3½ fl oz) milk
250 g (9 oz) strong white
  bread flour, plus extra for
  dusting
3 g (¾ tsp) salt
20 g (¾ oz/1 heaped tbsp)
  sugar
1 egg
60 g (2 oz) butter

Glaze

1 egg
3 tbsp milk

Tip

You can glaze your bao with
1 tablespoon of honey mixed
with 1 tablespoon of hot water
and sprinkle with grated lemon
zest and chopped coriander.

Filling

Chop the onion and press the garlic. Grate the carrot, but not too finely, then chop the candied lemon into small cubes. Slice the chicken into strips. Chop the coriander.

Heat the oil in a pan and sauté the onion. Add the carrot, season with salt and pepper and brown for 2 minutes. Leave to cool. Combine with the chicken and candied lemon, coriander, spices, pressed garlic and soy sauce. Set aside in the refrigerator. You can make the filling the day before.

Pastry

Mix the yeast with the milk. Sift the flour into a stand mixer. Add the salt, sugar and egg. Begin kneading using the dough hook. Add the milk and yeast mixture. Run for 10 minutes until the dough forms a ball that comes away from the sides. Add the diced butter. Knead until completely absorbed. The dough should be smooth and stretchy. As it turns, it should resemble a thread. The kneading should take around another 10 minutes. Cover with a dish towel and leave to rise for 1 hour at room temperature. Fold the dough (lift it up and then let it drop back down again), cover and leave in the refrigerator for 1 hour.

Folding & cooking

Weigh the dough and divide it into eight balls. Dust the work surface with flour and roll out the balls of dough, making sure the centre is thicker than the edges. Add one large spoonful of filling and start folding (page 132). Make sure you seal the buns well, then turn them over and arrange on a wire rack lined with baking parchment. Cover with a dish towel and leave to rise for 40 minutes.

Preheat the oven to 170°C (325°F/gas mark 3). For the glaze, whisk the egg and milk together in a bowl until combined. Glaze the bao using a pastry brush and bake in the oven for 25 minutes. Enjoy your bao buns as soon as they have cooled.

DIM SUM
DUMPLINGS & CO

**In Cantonese, dim sum literally
means 'touch your heart'.**

Dim sum are little bite-size snacks that used to be
served in tearooms to tempt caravanners travelling
along the Silk Road. In Guangdon, dim sum are only
served in the morning at 'yam tcha' (literally, 'drinking
tea'), which is like Chinese brunch.

PRAWN DUMPLINGS (HAR GAO OR HAKAO)

蝦餃

Makes **24 dumplings**
Preparation **1 hr 20 mins**
Chilling **20 mins**
Cooking **8–10 mins**

Filling
250 g (9 oz) raw prawns
  (shrimp), defrosted and
  shelled (280–300 g/10–
  10½ oz total)
50 g (2 oz) bamboo shoots,
  cut into strips (tinned)
1 heaped tbsp tapioca starch
1 large tbsp oyster sauce
1 tbsp soy sauce
1 tbsp sesame oil
2 tbsp rice wine (kwangtung
  mijiu)
1 tsp sugar
½ tsp salt
black pepper

Pastry
145 g (5 oz) wheat starch
35 g (1¼ oz) tapioca starch
200 ml (7 fl oz) boiling water
1 level tsp salt
2 tbsp vegetable oil

Tip
Har gao freeze very well.
Place them in a sealed
box, spaced apart, when
they are still fresh. Once they
are frozen, you can transfer
them to a bag so they take up
less space. In addition to the
thawing time, they will take
5 minutes to cook.

Filling

In a small saucepan, boil the bamboo shoots for 2 minutes to get rid of its acrid smell. Drain and pat dry. Roughly chop with a knife.

Chop half the prawns into small pieces. Mix the rest of the prawns with all the seasonings.

Combine the filling, bamboo shoots and chopped prawns.

You can heat a little of the filling in the microwave for 15 seconds to check the seasoning; adjust if necessary. Leave to rest in the refrigerator for 20 minutes before using. The filling can be prepared up to 2 days ahead; cover with cling film (plastic wrap) (in direct contact with the surface of the mixture) then chill.

Pastry

In a bowl, mix together the two starches and the salt. Make a well in the centre, pour in the oil, into the centre then add the boiling water, stirring with chopsticks or a wooden spatula. When the dough starts to blend together, pour it out onto a work surface and knead (while still hot) for 5 minutes with the palm of your hand. The dough will be hot but not boiling. The dough should be perfectly smooth, stretchy, soft and not sticky.

Folding & cooking

Roll out the dough into three logs. Wrap them in cling film to stop the dough from drying out. Cut into pieces weighing 15–17 g (½ oz). Cover with cling film. Roll out each piece of dough into a disc (with a diameter of 10–12 cm/4–4½ in). Use a pastry cutter to make perfect discs. Wrap the leftovers in cling film and keep; you can roll them out again later.

Make your har gao (page 136). When each one is ready, place It on a baking tray lined with baking sheet lined with baking parchment. Bring the water from the steamer to the boil. Cook for 8–10 minutes. Check the bottoms; there should not be any opaque patches, as this is a sign they are undercooked.

Enjoy straight away

Arrange the dumplings in a steamer basket, lined with baking parchment or salad leaves (without the veins).

You can serve your dumplings with chilli oil (page 116) or sriracha sauce (page 119) mixed with a dash of sesame oil.

HALF-MOON DUMPLINGS

WITH PORK & WOOD EAR MUSHROOMS (FUN GUO)
半月粉粿

Makes **24 dumplings**
Soaking: **15–20 mins**
Preparation **45 mins**
Chilling **20 mins**
Cooking **8–10 mins**

Filling
10 g (¼ oz) wood ear
   mushrooms
1 small onion
10 g (¼ oz) ginger
300 g (10½ oz) minced
   (ground) pork shoulder
1 tbsp sesame oil
1 tbsp tapioca starch or
   Maïzena®
2 tbsp soy sauce
¼ tsp salt
black pepper

Pastry
145 g (5 oz) wheat starch
35 g (1¼ oz) tapioca starch
200 ml (7 fl oz) boiling water
1 level tsp salt
2 tbsp vegetable oil

Tip
Like almost all dumplings, fun guo freeze very well. Place them in a sealed box when they are still fresh, spaced apart. Once they have frozen, you can transfer them to a bag so they take up less space. In addition to the thawing time, they will take 5 minutes to cook.

Filling
Soak the wood ear mushrooms in a container of hot water for 15–20 minutes. Chop the onion and grate the ginger. When the mushrooms are rehydrated, strain then roughly chop. Combine all the filling ingredients. Season generously with pepper and stir for 2–3 minutes: the filling should be slightly sticky. Chill for 20 minutes. You can make the filling up to 3 days in advance.

Pastry
In a container, combine both starches and the salt. Make a well in the centre and add the oil then pour in the boiling water, stirring with chopsticks or a wooden spatula. When the mixture starts to blend together, pour it out onto a work surface and knead for 5 minutes (while still hot) with the palm of your hand. The dough should be perfectly smooth, stretchy and not sticky.

Folding & cooking
Roll the dough out into three logs. Wrap with cling film (plastic wrap) to stop it from drying out. Cut into pieces weighing 15–17 g (½ oz) each. Wrap each one in cling film. Roll out each piece of dough into a disc (10–12 cm/ 4–4½ in in diameter). Use a pastry cutter to make perfect discs if you wish. Keep the leftovers wrapped in cling film; you can roll them out again later.

Add one spoonful of filling and fold the dough in two, pushing the air out to form a half moon. Press down firmly on the edges of the dough to seal up the dumpling. Repeat for the remaining dumplings.

Arrange in a steamer basket lined with baking parchment or salad leaves (without the veins). Bring the water in the steamer to the boil. Add the basket and cook for 8–10 minutes.

Enjoy straight away.

VEGGIE
CARROT, KOHLRABI & SHIITAKE
水晶素餃

Makes 15 dumplings
Soaking **1 night**
Preparation **45 mins**
Chilling **1 night**
Cooking **8–10 mins**

Filling
100 g (3½ oz) carrot
100 g (3½ oz) kohlrabi
20 g (¾ oz) dried shiitake
   mushrooms (9 small ones)
½ onion
½ bunch of coriander
   (cilantro)
10 g (¼ oz) fresh ginger root
2 garlic cloves
2 tbsp vegetable oil
2 tbsp soy sauce
1 tbsp oyster sauce
1 tsp sugar
black pepper

Pastry
100 g (3½ oz) wheat starch
80 g (3 oz) potato starch
150 ml (5 fl oz) boiling water
1 level tsp salt
2 tbsp vegetable oil

Filling

The day before, soak the shiitake mushrooms in a bowl of water. They need to be very soft. Alternatively, soak them in boiling water for at least 2 hours. The next day, finely dice the carrot and kohlrabi into 4 mm (⅛ in) cubes. When the shiitake mushrooms are rehydrated, strain and finely dice. Chop the onion and coriander, press the garlic, and grate the ginger. Heat the oil in a frying pan (skillet). Brown the onion and shiitake mushrooms for 5 minutes over a low heat. Add the ginger, garlic, vegetables, sauce and sugar. Season with pepper and continue cooking for a further 1–2 minutes. The vegetables should still be crunchy. Taste and adjust the seasoning as needed. Remove from the heat and add the coriander. Set aside. You can make the filling 1–2 days in advance.

Pastry

Combine both starches and the salt. Make a well in the centre, pour in the oil, then add the boiling water a little at a time, stirring with chopsticks or a spatula. When the dough starts to blend together, pour it out onto a work surface and knead for 5 minutes (while still hot). It should be nice and smooth.

Folding & cooking

Roll out the dough into three logs. Wrap with cling film (plastic wrap) to stop the dough from drying out. Cut into pieces weighing 20 g (¾ oz) each. Wrap in cling film. Roll out each piece of dough into a disc (with a diameter of 10–12 cm/4–4½ in). Use a pastry cutter to make perfect discs if you wish. Dollop 1 spoonful of filling onto the centre of each disc of dough. Fold like a bao (page 132). Pinch the dumplings to seal them well. Cut off any surplus dough with some scissors, then turn the dumpling over so the smooth side is on top. Repeat for the remaining dumplings. Arrange in a steamer basket lined with either baking parchment or salad leaves (without the veins). Bring the water in the steamer to the boil. Add the basket and cook for 8–10 minutes. Enjoy straight away.

PRAWN,
CELERIAC & SICHUAN PEPPER
花椒蝦餃

Makes **24 dumplings**
Preparation **1 hr**
Chilling **20 mins**
Cooking **8–10 mins**

Filling

1 tsp Sichuan pepper
250 g (9 oz) raw prawns
   (shrimp), defrosted and
   shelled (300 g/10½ oz total)
80 g (3 oz) celeriac (celery
   root)
1 heaped tbsp tapioca starch
1 large tbsp oyster sauce
1 tbsp soy sauce
1 tbsp Chilli Oil (page 116)
   or sesame oil
2 tbsp rice wine (kwangtung
   mijiu)
1 tsp sugar
½ tsp salt

Pastry

145 g (5 oz) wheat starch
35 g (1¼ oz) tapioca starch
1 level tsp salt
195 ml (7 fl oz water
1 tsp beetroot (beet) juice
2 tbsp vegetable oil

Filling

Grind the Sichuan pepper in a mortar or using a rolling pin. Finely dice the celeriac into 4 mm (⅛ in) cubes. Chop half the prawns into little pieces. Mix the rest of the prawns with all the seasonings.

Combine the mixed filling with the celeriac and chopped prawns.

You can heat a little of the filling in the microwave for 15 seconds to check the seasoning; adjust if necessary. Chill for 20 minutes before using.
You can prepare the filling up to 2 days in advance; cover with cling film (in direct contact with the surface of the mixture) and set aside in the refrigerator.

Pastry

In a large bowl, combine both starches and the salt. Make a well in the centre and add the oil. Bring the water mixed with the beet juice to the boil. Pour into the well a little at a time, stirring with chopsticks or a wooden spatula. When the dough starts to blend together, pour it out onto a work surface and knead for 5 minutes (while still hot) with the palm of your hand. The dough will be hot but not boiling. Your dough should be perfectly smooth, stretchy, soft and not sticky.

Folding & cooking

Roll the dough out into three logs. Wrap with cling film to stop it from drying out. Cut into pieces weighing 15–17 g (½ oz) each. Wrap in cling film. Roll out each piece of dough into a disc (with a diameter of 10–12 cm/4–4½ in). Use a pastry cutter to make perfect discs if you wish. Keep the leftovers; you can roll them out again later. Make the dumplings by folding them like a har gao (page 136). Set aside on a baking tray lined with baking parchment.

Arrange the dumplings in a steamer basket lined either with baking parchment or salad leaves (without the veins). Bring the water in the steamer to the boil. Add the basket and cook for 8–10 minutes.

Enjoy straight away.

SALMON,
MISO & GINGER
味噌鮭魚餃

Makes **24 dumplings**
Preparation **1 hr**
Chilling **2 hrs**
Cooking **8 mins**

Filling
400 g (14 oz) salmon fillet,
   skinned
15 g (½ oz) fresh ginger root
30 g (1 oz) white miso
2 tbsp saké or white wine
½ tsp sugar
1 small tbsp soy sauce

Pastry
230 ml (8 fl oz) water
100 g (3½ oz) spinach
145 g (5 oz) wheat starch
35 g (1¼ oz) tapioca starch

Filling

Chop the salmon into little 8 mm (⅜ in) cubes. Grate the ginger. Mix the miso with the saké, sugar and soy sauce. Add the ginger and salmon, then stir together. Chill for at least 2 hours, or ideally until the following day.

Pastry

Mix the water with the spinach using a hand-held blender. Weigh out 200 ml (7 fl oz) water, including the pulp. In a large bowl, combine both starches and the salt. Make a well and add the oil. Bring the green water mixture to the boil, then pour into the well a little at a time, stirring with chopsticks or a wooden spatula. When the dough starts to blend together, pour it out onto a work surface and knead (while still hot) for 5 minutes with the palm of your hand. The dough will be hot but not boiling. Your dough should be perfectly smooth, stretchy, soft and not sticky.

Folding & cooking

Roll out the dough into three logs. Wrap with cling film (plastic wrap) to stop it from drying out. Cut out into pieces weighing 15–17 g (½ oz) each. Wrap them with cling film. Roll out each piece of dough into a disc (10 cm/4 in in diameter). Use a pastry cutter to make perfect discs if you wish. Keep the leftovers wrapped in cling film; you can roll them out again later. Dollop one spoonful of salmon filling onto each disc of dough and fold into a half-moon shape, making sure you push the air out. Push down firmly to seal the dough and place the dumpling on its base so it stays upright. You can also make a fan-shaped fold (page 138). Set aside on a baking sheet lined with baking parchment.

Arrange the dumplings in steamer baskets lined either with baking paper or with salad leaves (without the veins). Bring the water in the steamer to the boil. Add the baskets and cook for 8 minutes. Enjoy straight away either on their own or with some coconut, miso & lime sauce (page 118).

COD, GINGER &
SPRING ONION
雙色鱈魚餃

Makes **22 dumplings**
Preparation **1 hr**
Chilling **20 mins**
Cooking **8–10 mins**

Filling
250 g (9 oz) cod fillet
2 spring onions (scallions)
  (70 g/2½ oz)
15 g (½ oz) fresh ginger root
1 heaped tbsp tapioca starch
1 egg white
1 large heaped tbsp oyster
  sauce
1 tbsp soy sauce
2 tbsp sesame oil
1 tbsp rice wine (kwangtung
  mijiu)
1 tsp sugar
½ tsp salt
black pepper

Green pastry
25 g (1 oz) spinach
120 ml (4 fl oz) water
70 g (2½ oz) wheat starch
20 g (¾ oz) tapioca starch
½ level tsp salt
1 tbsp vegetable oil

White pastry
70 g (2½ oz) wheat starch
20 g (¾ oz) tapioca starch
½ level tsp salt
1 tbsp vegetable oil
100 ml (3½ fl oz) boiling water

Filling

Chop half the cod into little cubes. Chop the green stalks of the spring onions. Finely slice the ginger and then dice. Mix the rest of the fish with the egg white, spring onions and all the seasonings. Combine the filling mixture with the diced cod, ginger and the green stalks of the spring onions. You can heat a little of the filling for 15 seconds in the microwave to check the seasoning; adjust if necessary. Chill for 20 minutes before using. You can make the filling the day before; cover with cling film (plastic wrap) (in direct contact with the surface of the mixture) and set aside in the refrigerator.

Pastries

Make the green pastry. Mix the spinach with the 120 ml (4 fl oz) water, either in a food processor or using a hand-held blender. Strain the mixture. You can add a bit of pulp to enhance the flavour.

In a large bowl, combine the two starches and the salt. Make a well in the centre and add the oil. Bring the green water mixture to the boil, then pour it into the well a little at a time, stirring with chopsticks or a wooden spatula. When the dough starts to blend together, pour it out onto a work surface and knead (while still hot) for 5 minutes with the palm of your hand. The dough will be hot but not boiling. It should be perfectly smooth, stretchy, soft, and not sticky. Cover the green pastry dough with cling film while you make the white pastry dough, following the same steps.

Folding & cooking

Roll the white dough out into an 18–20 cm (7–8 in) log. Roll out the green dough into a 24 x 12 cm (9½ x 4½ in) rectangle (page 150). Wrap the log in the green dough to make a two-coloured roll of dough. Cut into pieces weighing 16–18 g (½ oz) each. Wrap in cling film to stop the dough from drying out. Roll out each piece of dough into a disc (10–12 cm/4–4½ in in diameter). Use a pastry cutter to make perfect discs if you wish. Keep the leftovers wrapped in cling film; you can roll them out again later.

Dollop two spoonfuls of filling onto the centre of each disc of dough. Close the dumplings by folding into a half-moon shape. Press the sides together then fold the edge of the dough like a fan (page 138). Set aside on a baking sheet lined with baking parchment.

Arrange the dumplings in steamer baskets lined either with baking parchment or salad leaves (without the veins).

Bring the water in the steamer to the boil. Add the baskets and cook for 8–10 minutes. Enjoy straight away, either on their own or with a sauce of your choice (XO, black rice vinegar, coconut, miso & lime, sriracha).

COCONUT CHICKEN,
LIME & CORIANDER

椰香雞肉餃

Makes **25 dumplings**
Preparation **1 hr**
Chilling **20 mins**
Cooking **8–10 mins**

Filling

200 g (7 oz) chicken breast
100 ml (3½ fl oz) coconut milk
2 large shallots
2 tbsp vegetable oil
2 tbsp nuoc-mâm
1 level tsp sugar
¼ tsp salt
1 organic lime
6 sprigs of coriander
  (cilantro)
black pepper

Green pastry

50 g (2 oz) coriander
  (cilantro)
230 ml (8 fl oz) water
145 g (5 oz) wheat starch
35 g (1¼ oz) tapioca starch
1 level tsp salt
2 tbsp vegetable oil

Filling

Slice the chicken with a knife. Chop the shallots and coriander. Heat the oil in a small saucepan and fry the shallots until golden brown. Add the coconut milk, sugar, nuoc-mâm and salt. Stir and reduce for 5 minutes.

Leave to cool before mixing with the chicken. Add the chopped coriander and lime zest and squeeze in half the juice. Stir and set aside in the refrigerator while you make the pastry.

Green pastry

Roughly chop the coriander, including the stalks. Mix with the water using a food processor or hand-held blender. Strain and weigh out 200 ml (7 fl oz).

You can add a bit of coriander pulp to enhance the flavour. In a bowl, combine both starches and the salt. Make a well and add the oil. Bring the green water mixture to the boil then pour it into the well a little at a time, stirring with chopsticks or a wooden spatula. When the dough starts to blend together, pour it out onto a work surface and knead (while still hot) for 5 minutes with the palm of your hand. The dough will be warm but not boiling hot. Your pastry dough should be perfectly smooth, stretchy and soft and should not stick to your hands.

Folding & cooking

Roll out the dough into three logs. Wrap with cling film to stop the dough from drying out. Cut into pieces weighing 15–17 g (½ oz) each. Wrap them in cling film. Roll out each piece of dough into a disc (10–12 cm/4–4½ in in diameter). Use a pastry cutter to make perfect discs if you wish. Wrap the leftovers in cling film and set aside; you can roll them out again later.

Dollop one spoonful of filling onto the centre of each disc of dough. Fold two edges towards the centre, then fold over the opposite side to form a three-cornered hat and pinch the edges together to seal (page 140).

Place the dumplings in steamer baskets and cook for 8–10 minutes (from the moment the water comes to the boil). Serve with a little dash of lime juice or coconut, miso & lime sauce (page 118).

PORK SHUMAI (XIU MAI)

燒賣

Makes **30 shumai**
(bite-size dumplings)
Preparation **1 hr**
Chilling time **20 mins**
Cooking **8-10 mins**

Filling

1 onion
100 g (3½ oz) water
  chestnuts
chives
20 g (¾ oz) fresh ginger root
500 g (1 lb 2 oz) minced
  (ground) pork shoulder
8 spring onions (scallions)
2 tbsp rice wine
2 tbsp soy sauce
2 tbsp sesame oil
½ tsp salt
2 tbsp tapioca flour
1 egg white

Pastry

1 packet of wonton pastry
  wrappers (sold fresh)

Tip

Once you have assembled
your bite-size dumplings, you
can freeze them. Cook them
for 12-15 minutes without
thawing.

Filling

Chop the onion and strain and finely dice the chestnuts. Chop the chives and grate the ginger. In a large bowl, combine all the filling ingredients. You can heat up a little of the filling in the microwave for 15 seconds to check the seasoning; adjust if necessary. Set aside in the refrigerator for at least 20 minutes. Ideally, prepare the day before.

Folding & cooking

Separate the wonton wrappers. Dollop 1 large teaspoon of filling onto the centre of a wrapper. Moisten the edges with a little water, then pull the pastry over the filling. Pick up the dumpling in your hand and press down lightly to seal the filling and create your dumpling. Press down on the top with a little spatula or butter knife. The pastry should perfectly encased around the filling.

Arrange in steamer baskets and cook for 8-10 minutes (from the moment the water comes to the boil). Enjoy straight away with a bit of sriracha sauce (page 119) or chilli oil (page 116).

SOUP DUMPLINGS (XIALONG BAO)
小籠包

Makes **32 dumplings**
Preparation **1 hr 30 mins**
Chilling **1 night**
Cooking **8 mins**

Filling

300 g (10½ oz) minced
   (ground) pork shoulder
30 g (1 oz) onion, finely
   choppped
15 g (½ oz) ginger, grated
50 ml (1¾ fl oz/3 tbsp)
   chicken stock
2 tbsp soy sauce
1 tbsp sesame oil
1 tbsp Shaoxing wine
   (optional)
1 level tsp salt
1 level tsp sugar
black pepper

Jelly

200 ml (7 fl oz) chicken stock
½ tsp agar-agar

Pastry

200 g (7 oz) strong white
   bread flour, plus extra for
   dusting
½ tsp salt
120 ml (4 fl oz) boiling water

Sauce

10 g (¼ oz) fresh ginger root
black rice vinegar (yonghun
   laogu)

Jelly & filling

The day before, for the jelly, whisk the stock and agar-agar together in a small saucepan. Boil for about a minute, then pour into a little dish or bowl. Leave in the refrigerator to set overnight. Combine all the filling ingredients, stirring until the stock has been absorbed and the mixture turns slightly sticky. Cover with cling film (plastic wrap) (in direct contact with the surface of the mixture) and chill overnight.

The following day, chop the jelly into little cubes and mix with the filling. Set aside in the refrigerator while you make the pastry.

Pastry

Mix the flour and salt together in a large bowl. Make a well in the centre, then pour in the boiling water, stirring with a spatula or chopsticks. When the dough starts to turn lumpy, knead for 5 minutes until it all blends together. Pour out onto a work surface and continue kneading for a few minutes. The dough should be smooth and stretchy.

Folding & cooking

Roll out the dough into two logs, then cut into little 10 g (¼ oz) pieces. Cover them with cling film to stop the dough from drying out. Dust the work surface with flour and roll the pieces of dough out into discs with a diameter of 10 cm (4 in). Use a pastry cutter to make perfect discs if you wish. Dollop 1 teaspoon of filling onto the centre of each disc. Make the folds (page 148). Bring all the folds together, pinch and turn over to seal the dumpling. If you notice there is too much dough while you are pinching, cut off any excess and pinch to make another little tip. Make sure you seal up the centre well to top the broth from leaking out while cooking.

Arrange in steamer baskets lined with baking parchment (if this is what you generally use). Alternatively, set aside in the refrigerator on a dish lined with baking parchment while you make the remaining dumplings. The pastry for xiaolong bao is thin and the broth may start to go soft.

Cook the dumplings for 8 minutes (from the moment the water comes to the boil). Slice the ginger for the sauce into very fine julienne strips. Serve straight away with black rice vinegar mixed with the sliced ginger.

Enjoy!

Pour a little black rice vinegar and ginger onto a spoon. Pick up a dumpling using chopsticks and drop it onto the spoon. Make a hole with your chopsticks and let the juice flow out. Blow on it a little to cool it down then gobble down your xiaolong bao in one delicious mouthful!

MUSHROOM
& SMOKED DUCK BREAST FILLET
帕馬森鴨胸餃

Makes **20 dumplings**
Preparation **30 mins**
Cooking **5–6 mins**

Filling
300 g (10½ oz) button
  mushrooms
1 shallot
1 large garlic clove
4 sprigs of flat-leaf parsley
90 g (3¼ oz) smoked duck
  breast
20 g (¾ oz) Parmesan
1 tbsp olive oil
salt and black pepper

Pastry
1 packet of wonton pastry
  wrappers (sold fresh)

Filling

Wash the mushrooms then chop. Chop the shallot, garlic and parsley. Remove the fat from the duck breast fillet and save for later. Cut the slices into cubes. Grate the Parmesan.

In a frying pan (skillet), heat the oil with the duck fat. Brown the shallot, then add the mushrooms and cook until nicely browned. Remove from the heat and add the garlic, parsley, duck breast fillet and Parmesan. Season with pepper, mix, and taste. Add salt if needed.

Folding & cooking

Make your dumplings. Separate the wonton wrappers. Moisten the edges with water using a pastry brush. Spoon a little of the filling onto the centre and fold into the shape of a fish (page 144). For an easier fold, you can also just fold the pastry diagonally to form a triangle. Arrange in a steamer basket lined with baking parchment and cook for 5–6 minutes. Enjoy straight away with a salad, if liked.

FRIED PRAWN
DUMPLINGS
炸蝦餃

Makes **24 dumplings**
Preparation **30 mins**
Cooking **2 mins**

Filling
300 g (10½ oz) raw prawns
  (shrimp), defrosted and
  shelled (350 g/12 oz total)
50 g (2 oz) water chestnuts
  or ½ carrot
½ onion
1 egg white
1 tbsp Maïzena®
1 tsp sugar
1 large tbsp oyster sauce
½ tsp salt
black pepper

Pastry
1 packet of wonton pastry
  wrappers (sold fresh)

Spicy mayonnaise
1 egg white
150 ml (5 fl oz) neutral oil
50 ml (1¾ fl oz/3 tbsp) Chilli
  Oil
1 heaped tsp mustard
1 tbsp lemon juice
1 garlic clove
salt

Cooking
1 litre (34 fl oz) cooking oil

Filling

Chop the onion and finely dice the water chestnuts or carrot. Chop half the prawns into small pieces. Mix the rest of the prawns with the egg white, Maïzena®, sugar, oyster sauce and salt. The mixture should turn slightly sticky.

Pour the filling into a salad bowl and add the onion, remaining prawns and the water chestnuts or carrot. Season with pepper and stir. You can heat up little of the filling in the microwave for 15 seconds to check the seasoning; adjust if necessary.

Folding

Fill a little bowl with water. Separate the wonton pastry wrappers. Dollop 1 tablespoon of filling onto the centre of each wrapper. Moisten the edges, join together two opposite corners (diagonally) and close like a bag (page 138). Set aside on a dish lined with baking parchment.

Spicy mayonnaise

In a bowl, combine the egg white, mustard, pressed garlic clove, lemon juice and a pinch of salt. Begin whisking using an electric whisk. When the mixture starts to thicken, pour in the neutral oil a little at a time, whisking constantly. Wait until the oil has been absorbed before adding more. Once the mayonnaise has set, add the chilli oil, continuing to whisk. Taste and adjust the seasoning if necessary. Set aside in the refrigerator.

Cooking

Heat the oil in a deep frying pan (skillet) until it reaches 180°C (350°F). Drop a few dumplings in and brown for 2 minutes. Pat dry on paper towels. Repeat with several batches. Serve straight away with the spicy mayonnaise.

CRAB
WITH LEMONGRASS & COCONUT SOUP
蟹肉椰汁湯餃

Makes **30 dumplings /
serves 4**
Preparation **45 mins**
Cooking **2 mins**

Filling
½ onion
80 g (3 oz) water chestnuts
   (tinned)
½ bunch of coriander
   (cilantro)
150 g (5 oz) minced (ground)
   pork (belly or shoulder)
150 g (5 oz) crab meat
1 tbsp soy sauce
1 level tsp salt
1 level tsp sugar
1 tbsp tapioca starch
   or Maïzena®

Pastry
1 packet of wonton pastry
   wrappers (sold fresh)

Coconut & lemongrass
soup
1 litre (34 fl oz) chicken stock
   or water
25 g (1 oz) red Thai curry
   paste (strength according
   to your preference)
4 lemongrass stalks
10 makrut lime leaves, frozen
4 tbsps nuoc-mâm
1 level tsp sugar
500 ml (17 fl oz) coconut milk

To serve
½ bunch of coriander
   (cilantro), leaves only
1 lime

Filling
Chop the onion and finely dice the water chestnuts. Chop the coriander. Combine all the filling ingredients. Set aside in the refrigerator while you make the soup.

Coconut & lemongrass soup
Remove the tough parts from the lemongrass. Cut the stalks into thin slices so the flavour infuses better. In a saucepan, combine the chicken stock, lemongrass, red curry paste and makrut lime leaves. Bring to the boil. Reduce the heat and add the sugar and nuoc-mâm. Leave to infuse for 10 minutes over a low heat, then add the coconut milk. Taste and adjust the seasoning if necessary. Set aside.

Folding
Fill a small bowl with water. Separate the wonton pastry wrappers. Dollop 1 tablespoon of filling onto the centre of each wrapper. Moisten the edges, join two opposite corners together in the shape of a bag (page 138). Set aside on a dish lined with baking parchment.

Cooking
Bring some water to the boil in a large saucepan. Heat up the coconut & lemongrass soup in another saucepan.

Drop the dumplings into the boiling water and cook for 2–3 minutes. They should rise to the surface. Strain and divide into bowls. Pour in the hot broth. Serve with coriander leaves and a dash of lime juice.

GOLDEN CHICKEN
MONEY BAGS
雞肉福袋

Makes **30 money bags**
Soaking **10 mins**
Preparation **45 mins**
Cooking **2 mins**

Filling
250 g (9 oz) chicken breast
½ onion
½ carrot
5 g (⅛ oz) dried wood ear
   mushrooms
1 level tsp salt
1 level tsp sugar
½ bunch of coriander
black pepper

Pastry
30 chives
1 packet of wonton pastry
   wrappers (sold fresh)

Cooking
1 litre (34 fl oz) cooking oil

Filling

Soak the mushrooms in boiling water for 10 minutes.

Roughly chop the chicken using a knife. Chop the onion and coriander and grate the carrot. Roughly chop the rehydrated, strained mushrooms. Combine all the ingredients with the chicken, then add the sugar, salt and generous amounts of pepper.

Folding

Bring some water to the boil in a saucepan and blanch the chives for 5 seconds. Strain, rinse in cold water and strain again. Fill a small bowl with water. Separate the wonton pastry wrappers. Dollop 1 tablespoon of filling onto the centre of each sheet. Moisten the edges, join together the four corners and close up to make an 'aumoniere' (money bag). Pinch the centre together firmly to seal the pastry. Tie together with 1 chive. Set aside on a dish lined with baking paper.

Cooking

Heat the oil in a deep frying pan (skillet) until it reaches 180°C (350°F). Drop in a few money bags and brown for 2 minutes. Pat dry with paper towels. Repeat with several batches. Enjoy straight away either on their own or with store-bought sweet chilli sauce.

PEKING
PORK & CHINESE CABBAGE
白菜豬肉鍋貼

Makes **30 dumplings**
Preparation **1 hr**
Chilling **20 mins**
Cooking **15 mins**

Filling
150 g (5 oz) Chinese cabbage
1 small onion
20 g (¾ oz) fresh ginger root
400 g (14 oz) pork shoulder
   or minced (ground) pork
1 level tsp sugar
2 tbsp soy sauce
½ tsp salt
black pepper

Pastry
300 g (10½ oz) strong white
   bread flour
½ tsp salt
170 ml (6 fl oz) boiling water

Cooking
vegetable oil

To create crispy, lace-like dumplings
Add 1 tbsp of flour to the
water used for cooking the
dumplings.

Tip
You can substitute the
Chinese cabbage with 120 g
(4 oz) chopped garlic chives
or wild garlic.

Filling

Cut the cabbage leaves in three then blanch for 3 minutes in a pan of salted boiling water. Drain and leave to cool.

Chop the onion and grate the ginger. Squeeze the cabbage firmly between your hands to get rid of the water then chop. Combine all the vegetables with the meat and add the seasonings. You can heat up a little of the filling in the microwave for 15 seconds to check the seasoning; adjust if necessary. Chill for 20 minutes.

Pastry

Combine the flour and salt in a large bowl, then make a well in the centre. Pour in the boiling water, stirring with a spatula or chopsticks. When the dough starts to turn lumpy, knead for 5 minutes to blend it all together. Pour out onto a work surface and continue kneading for a few minutes. The dough should be smooth and stretchy.

Folding

Roll out the dough into three logs. Cut into small 15 g (½ oz) pieces and wrap in cling film (plastic wrap) or cover with a dish towel to stop the dough from drying out.

Dust the work surface with flour and roll out the pieces of dough into discs (10–12 cm/4–4½ in in diameter). Use a pastry cutter to make perfect discs if you wish. Keep the leftovers wrapped in cling film; you can roll them out again later.

Dollop one spoonful of filling onto the middle of a disc of dough and join up two opposite sides of the disc in the centre (page 142). Pinch lightly so they stick together. Make three to four folds on the right, starting at the centre, then three to four on the left. Pinch the edges each time to seal up the dough. Set aside on a dish lined with baking parchment.

Cooking

Cook in 2 batches or freeze some of the dumplings. Heat 2 tablespoons of oil in a 28 cm (11 in) non-stick frying pan. Add half the dumplings, making sure they're not too close together; they should not be touching. Sizzle for a few minutes before adding some water – the water should reach up to about two-thirds of the height of the dumplings (around 220 ml (7½ fl oz). Cover and continue cooking until the water has evaporated.

Uncover and toast the bottoms of the dumplings, checking to see if they are cooked. The dumplings are done when they are nicely browned underneath. Repeat with the remaining dumplings, washing the pan in between each batch. Serve straight away with black rice vinegar and shredded ginger, or with the sauce of your choice: chilli oil, XO sauce, etc.

PORK,
SICHUAN PEPPER & DAN DAN SAUCE
川味擔擔豬肉餃

Makes **20 dumplings**
Preparation **45 mins**
Chilling **20 mins**
Cooking **10–12 mins**

Filling
½ onion
1 garlic clove
20 g (¾ oz) fresh ginger root
1 level tsp Sichuan pepper
250 g (9 oz) minced (ground)
  pork belly or shoulder
1 level tsp sugar
2 tbsp soy sauce
½ tsp salt
30 g (1 oz) fermented
  mustard greens

Pastry
250 g (9 oz) strong white
  bread flour
½ tsp salt
150 ml (5 fl oz) boiling water

Dan dan sauce
80 g (3 oz) tahini
10 g (¼ oz/2½ tsp) sugar
30 ml (1 fl oz/2 tbsp) hot
  water
50 ml (1¾ fl oz/3 tbsp)
  Chinkiang black rice vinegar
50 ml (1¾ fl oz/3 tbsp) soy
  sauce
Chilli Oil (page 116)

To serve
2 chives
50 g (2 oz) roasted peanuts

Filling

Chop the onion, press the garlic and grate the ginger. Crush the Sichuan pepper either in a mortar or with a rolling pin. Combine with the minced pork and the seasonings and mustard greens (if you are using kimchi, chop roughly first). Set aside in the refrigerator for 20 minutes.

Pastry

Combine the flour and salt in a large bowl, then make a well in the centre. Pour in the boiling water, stirring with a spatula or chopsticks. When the pastry starts to blend together, pour it out onto a work surface and knead for 5 minutes until smooth and stretchy.

Folding & cooking

Roll out the dough into three logs. Cut into little 15–18 g (½ oz) pieces and wrap them in cling film (plastic wrap) or cover with a dish towel to stop the dough from drying out.

Dust a work surface with flour and roll out the pieces of dough into discs (10–11 cm/4–4¼ in in diameter). For perfect discs, use a pastry cutter. Dollop one spoonful of filling onto the centre of each disc of dough and fold into the shape of a three-cornered hat (page 140).

Arrange the dumplings in a steamer lined with baking parchment. When the water comes to the boil, add the basket and cook for 10–12 minutes.

Dan dan sauce & presentation

Chop the chives and grind the peanuts. For the sauce, mix the tahini with the sugar in a bowl, then add the hot water. Mix with the vinegar and soy sauce. Add the chilli oil, to taste. Serve the dumplings with the sauce, sprinkled with chives and peanuts.

Tip

Mustard greens are sold pre-chopped in little vacuum-packed bags.

BEEF, SESAME & CELERY

香芹牛肉鍋貼

Makes **24 raviolis**
Preparation **45 mins**
Chilling **20 mins**
Cooking **10 mins**

Filling
½ onion
20 g (¾ oz) fresh ginger root
150 g (5 oz) celery stalks
250 g (9 oz) minced (ground)
    beef
2 tbsp soy sauce
½ tsp salt
1 tbsp sesame oil
black pepper

Beetroot pastry
250 g (9 oz) strong white
    bread flour
½ tsp salt
90 ml (3 fl oz/6 tbsp) water
60 ml (2 fl oz) beetroot (beet)
    juice

Cooking
vegetable oil

Filling

Chop the onion, grate the ginger and finely dice the celery stalks. Combine with the minced beef and seasonings and add generous amounts of pepper. Set aside in the refrigerator for 20 minutes.

Beetroot pastry

Combine the flour and salt in a large bowl, then make a well in the centre. Bring the water and beetroot juice to the boil. Pour into the well, stirring with a spatula or chopsticks. When the dough starts to turn lumpy, knead for 5 minutes until it has all blended together. Pour it out onto the work surface and continue kneading for a few minutes. The dough should be smooth and stretchy.

Folding

Roll out the dough into three logs. Cut into little 16–18 g (½ oz) pieces and wrap in cling film (plastic wrap) or cover with a clean dish towel to stop the dough from drying out. Dust the work surface with flour and roll out the pieces into discs (10 cm/4 in in diameter). For perfect discs, use a pastry cutter. Dollop 1 spoonful of filling onto the centre of each disc of dough, then fold in the shape of Peking dumplings (page 142). Arrange the dumplings on a dish lined with baking parchment.

Cooking

Cook in two batches. Heat 2 tablespoons of oil in a 28 cm (11 in) non-stick lidded frying pan (skillet). Add half the dumplings, making sure they are not too close together. They should not be touching. Sizzle for a few minutes before adding some water; it should reach up to around one-third of the height of the dumplings (about 220 ml/7½ fl oz). Cover with a lid and cook until the water has evaporated. Uncover and toast the bottoms, checking to see if they are cooked. The dumplings are done when they are nicely browned underneath. Repeat with the remaining dumplings, washing the pan in between each batch.

You can serve your dumplings with some dan dan sauce, XO sauce, black vinegar sauce, or just some soy sauce.

PORK,
GINGER & XO SAUCE
XO醬豬肉餃

Makes **20 dumplings**
Preparation **45 mins**
Chilling **20 mins**
Cooking **10–12 mins**

Filling
½ onion
1 garlic clove
20 g (¾ oz) fresh ginger root
250 g (9 oz) minced (ground)
    pork belly or shoulder
1 level tsp sugar
2 tbsp soy sauce
½ tsp salt
black pepper

Pastry
250 g (9 oz) strong white
    bread flour
½ tsp salt
150 ml (5 fl oz) boiling water

To serve
XO Sauce (page 117)

Filling

Chop the onion, press the garlic and grate the ginger. Combine with the minced pork and the seasonings. Season generously with pepper. Set aside in the refrigerator for 20 minutes.

Pastry

Combine the flour and salt in a large bowl, then make a well in the centre. Pour in the boiling water, stirring with a spatula or chopsticks. When the dough starts to blend together, pour it out onto a work surface and knead for 5 minutes until it is smooth and stretchy.

Folding & cooking

Roll the dough out into three balls. Cut into little 15–18 g (½ oz) pieces and wrap in cling film (plastic wrap) or cover with a clean dish towel to stop the dough from drying out. Dust the work surface with flour and roll out the pieces into 10–12 cm (4–4½ in) discs. For perfect discs use a pastry cutter. Dollop one spoonful of filling onto the centre of each disc of dough. Fold into the shape of a leaf (page 146). Arrange the dumplings in a steamer basket lined with baking parchment. When the water comes to the boil, add the basket and cook for 10–12 minutes. Serve the dumplings with the XO sauce. You can add some coriander leaves, chopped spring onions and chopped peanuts, if liked.

CHICKEN, SPINACH &
WOOD EAR MUSHROOM MONEY BAGS

波菜雞肉福袋

Makes **30 money bags**
Soaking **15 mins**
Preparation **45 mins**
Cooking **5–7 mins**

Filling
5 g (⅛ oz) dried wood ear
    mushrooms
½ onion
2 garlic cloves
150 g (5 oz) chicken
200 g (7 oz) spinach
2 tbsp vegetable oil
1 tbsp oyster sauce
1 tbsp soy sauce
½ tsp salt
1 tbsp sesame oil
black pepper

Pastry
1 packet of gyoza pastry
    wrappers

Filling

Rehydrate the wood ear mushrooms by soaking them in a bowl of hot water for 15 minutes. Chop the onion and press the garlic. Chop the chicken. When the mushrooms are rehydrated, strain, remove the hard parts if necessary and roughly chop.

Blanch the spinach for 30 seconds in a pan of salted boiling water. Strain. Leave to cool then squeeze between your hands to get rid of all the water. Chop roughly.

Heat the vegetable oil in a frying pan (skillet). Brown the onion and garlic. Add the chicken and all the seasonings and stir together. Add the wood ear mushrooms and continue cooking for 1 minute. Remove from the heat and add the spinach and sesame oil. Mix well, then leave to cool down completely. Taste and adjust the seasoning if necessary.

Folding & cooking

Separate the gyoza wrappers. Dollop a little of the filling onto the centre of a wrapper. Moisten the edges with a bit of water then pull the wrapper together in the centre to make a pouch. Pinch the centre firmly under the folds to seal up your money bag.

Arrange the money bags in a steamer basket lined with baking parchment or with salad leaves (without the veins). Cook for 5–7 minutes (from the point of the water coming to the boil). The money bags are cooked when the pastry on the surface is stretchy. Serve straight away.

VEGGIE
TOFU, CARROT, MUSHROOM & KIMCHI
泡菜素餃

Makes **30 dumplings**
Preparation **45 mins**
Cooking **5 mins**

Filling
1 carrot
140 g (5 oz) shiitake
  or button mushrooms
140 g (5 oz) kimchi
2 tbsp vegetable oil
200 g (7 oz) firm tofu
½ tsp sugar
3 tbsp soy sauce

Pastry
1 packet of gyoza wrappers
  (check the number of
  wrappers)

Filling

Finely dice the carrot, mushrooms and kimchi. Heat the oil in a frying pan (skillet). Brown the carrot and mushrooms for 5 minutes until the vegetables are browned. Break up the tofu into crumbs by hand. Add the tofu, kimchi and seasonings. Mix well.

Folding & cooking

Fill a small bowl with water. Dollop one spoonful of filling onto the centre of a pastry wrapper. Moisten the edges and fold in the shape of a fish (page 144). Remove the air and pinch the pastry together to seal the edges.

Arrange the dumplings in steamer baskets lined with baking parchment. Bring the water in the steamer to the boil, add the dumplings and cook for 5 minutes. The pastry should be stretchy. Serve with the sauce of your choice.

PORK BELLY
& KIMCHI
泡菜豬肉餃

Makes **30 dumplings**
Preparation **45 mins**
Chilling **20 mins**
Cooking **15 mins**

Filling
140 g (5 oz) kimchi
1 garlic clove
20 g (¾ oz) fresh ginger root
250 g (9 oz) minced (ground)
   pork belly or shoulder
1 level tsp sugar
2 tbsp soy sauce
2 tbsp sesame oil

Pastry
300 g (10½ oz) strong white
   bread flour
½ tsp salt
170 ml (6 fl oz) water kimchi

Cooking
vegetable oil

Sauce
3 tbsp soy sauce
1 tbsp sesame oil
1 tsp toasted sesame seeds
1 spring onion (scallion),
   chopped

Tip
To make the pastry lace-thin
and crisp, mix 1 tablespoon of
rice flour with the water used
for cooking the dumplings.

Filling
Strain the kimchi and set the fermentation water aside for the pastry. Roughly chop the kimchi, press the garlic and grate the ginger. Combine with the meat, seasonings and egg in a large bowl. Leave in the refrigerator for 20 minutes while you make the pastry.

Pastry
Measure 170 ml (5.4 fl oz) of the reserved kimchi water, adding extra water to make up the weight, if necessary. Combine the flour and salt in a large bowl, then make a well in the centre. Bring the kimchi water to the boil, then pour into the well, stirring with a spatula or chopsticks. When the dough starts to blend together, pour it out onto a work surface and knead for 5 minutes until soft and stretchy.

Folding & cooking
Roll the dough out into three logs. Cut into little 18–20 g (¾ oz) pieces and cover in cling film (plastic wrap) or with a clean dish towel, to stop the dough from drying out. Dust the work surface with flour and roll out the pieces into 10 cm (4 in) discs. Use a pastry cutter to make perfect discs. Dollop a spoonful of filling onto the centre of each disc of dough. Fold into a pyramid shape (page 140). Heat 2 tablespoons of vegetable oil in a non-stick frying pan. Place some of the dumplings in the pan, making sure they are not too close together; they should not be touching. Sizzle for a few minutes before adding water up to half the height of the dumplings (around 220 ml/7½ fl oz). Cover and cook until the water has evaporated. Remove the lid and toast the bottoms of the dumplings, checking to see if they are cooked. The dumplings are done when they are nicely browned underneath. Repeat with the remaining dumplings, washing the frying pan in between each batch.

Sauce
Combine all the sauce ingredients and serve with the dumplings.

CURRY
LEMONGRASS & MAKRUT PORK
咖喱香茅豬肉餃

Makes **30 dumplings**
Preparation **1 hr**
Chilling **20 mins**
Cooking **15 mins**

Filling
70 g (2½ oz) bamboo shoots
5 makrut lime leaves
1 lemongrass stalk (20 g/
 ¾ oz)
1 shallot
10 g (¾ oz) Thai red curry
 paste (1 level tbsp)
1 tbsp nuoc-mam
250 g (9 oz) minced (ground)
 pork belly or shoulder
1 level tsp sugar
½ tsp salt

Pastry
300 g (10½ oz) strong white
 bread flour
½ tsp salt
1 slightly heaped tbsp paprika
170 ml (6 fl oz) boiling water

Cooking
vegetable oil

Filling

Boil the bamboo shoots for 1 minute in a saucepan of water to get rid of their acrid smell. Strain. Remove the hard stalks from the makrut lime leaves. Roll them up, then chop very finely. Remove the hard parts from the lemongrass, then chop very finely. Chop the shallot.

Thin down the curry paste by mixing with the nuoc-mâm. Combine all the filling ingredients in a large bowl. You can heat up a little of the filling in the microwave for 15 seconds to check the seasoning; adjust if necessary. Leave to chill in the refrigerator for 20 minutes.

Pastry

Combine the flour, salt and paprika in a large bowl and make a well in the centre. Pour in the boiling water, stirring with a spatula or chopsticks. When the pastry starts to blend together, pour it out onto a work surface and knead for 5 minutes until smooth and stretchy.

Folding

Roll out the dough into three logs. Cut into little pieces weighing 18–20 g (¾ oz) each and cover with cling film (plastic wrap) or with a clean dish towel, to stop the dough from drying out. Dust the work surface with flour and roll out the pieces into 10–11 cm (4–4¼ in) discs. Use a pastry cutter to make perfect discs. Dollop a spoonful of filling onto the centre of each disc of dough. Fold into the shape of a leaf (page 146). Set aside on a plate.

Cooking

Cook in two batches or freeze some of the dumplings. Heat 2 tablespoons of oil in a 28 cm (11 in) non-stick lidded frying pan (skillet). Add half of the dumplings to the pan, making sure they are not too close together; they should not be touching. Sizzle for a few minutes before adding water up to half the height of the dumplings. Cover with a lid and cook until the water has evaporated. Remove the lid and toast the bottoms of the dumplings, checking to see if they are cooked. The dumplings are done when they are nicely browned underneath. Repeat for the remaining dumplings, washing the frying pan in between each batch. These dumplings do not need any sauce. If you want, you can add a little dash of lime juice.

PRAWN
& ASPARAGUS
雙色鮮蝦蘆筍餃

Makes **20 dumplings**
Preparation **1 hr**
Cooking **12 mins**

Filling
5 button mushrooms
2 garlic cloves
2 thin green asparagus
  (60 g/2 oz)
1 tbsp vegetable oil
50 g (2 oz) bacon lardons
250 g (9 oz) raw prawns
  (shrimp), defrosted and
  shelled (300 g/10½ oz total)
1 large tbsp oyster sauce
1 tbsp soy sauce
2 tbsp white wine
1 tsp sugar
½ tsp salt
black pepper

Pink pastry
125 g (4 oz) strong white
  bread flour, sifted, plus
  extra for dusting
¼ tsp salt
70 ml (2½ fl oz/scant
  5 tbsp) water
5 ml (1 tsp) beetroot juice

White pastry
125 g (4 oz) strong white
  bread flour
¼ tsp salt
75 ml (2½ fl oz/5 tbsp) boiling
  water

Filling

Wash the mushrooms and cut into cubes. Press the garlic. Finely dice the asparagus. Heat the oil in a frying pan (skillet) and brown the bacon lardons. When they start to brown, add the mushrooms and cook until the mushrooms are slightly browned. Remove from the heat and add the garlic and diced asparagus. Mix and leave to cool. Cut half of the prawns into pieces. Mix the rest with the seasonings. Mix both types of prawns and the sautéed mushrooms with the asparagus. Set aside in the refrigerator while you make the pastry.

Pastries

To make the pink pastry, combine the flour and salt in a large bowl. Make a well in the centre. Bring the water and beetroot juice to the boil. Pour into the well a little at a time, stirring with a spatula or chopsticks. When the dough starts to blend together, pour it out onto a work surface and knead for 5 minutes until it is smooth and stretchy. Roll out into a log 26 cm (10½ in) long and cover with cling film (plastic wrap) or a clean dish towel to stop the pastry from drying out. Repeat to make the white pastry. When it is nice and smooth, roll it out into a rectangle measuring 28 x 16 cm (11 x 6¼ in) (page 150). Wrap the pink log in the white pastry dough, creating a roll. Cut the roll in half, then stretch out each log to reduce its diameter. Cut into pieces weighing 18–20 g (¾ oz) each and wrap in cling film.

Folding & cooking

Dust the work surface with flour and roll out the pieces into 10–12 cm (4–4½ in) discs. Use a pastry cutter to make perfect discs. Dollop a spoonful of filling onto the centre of each disc of dough. Fold into the shape of a leaf (page 146). Steam-cook the dumplings for 12 minutes. Serve with the sauce(s) of your choice.

COD & CHORIZO

墨汁鱈魚餃

Makes **25 dumplings**
Preparation **1 hr**
Cooking **12–15 mins**

Filling
1 onion
1 large garlic clove
80 g (3 oz) spicy chorizo
1 tbsp olive oil, plus extra
2 small sprigs of thyme
300 g (10½ oz) cod fillet
3 sprigs or flat-leaf parsley
salt and black pepper

Black pastry
250 g (9 oz) strong white
    bread flour, plus extra for
    dusting
½ tsp salt
8 ml (scant 2 tsp) cuttlefish
    ink
150 ml (5 fl oz) boiling water

Tip
To make the pastry lace-thin
and crisp, add 1 tablespoon
of rice flour to the water you
use for cooking the dumplings.
Stir well before pouring into
the frying pan.

Filling

Chop the onion and press the garlic. Cut up the chorizo into small cubes.

Heat the oil in a frying pan (skillet) and brown the chorizo. When it starts to release its oil, add the onion, garlic and thyme and brown for 5 minutes. Leave to cool.

Blend the cod until it becomes a slightly sticky paste. Transfer to a salad bowl and add the onion and chorizo mixture, as well as the chopped parsley. Season lightly. You can heat up a little of the filling in the microwave for 15 seconds to check the seasoning; adjust if necessary. Set aside in the refrigerator while you make the pastry and the discs.

Black pastry

Combine the flour and salt in a large bowl. Make a well in the centre, then pour in the cuttlefish ink. Pour in the boiling water, stirring with a spatula or chopsticks. When the dough starts to turn lumpy, knead for 5 minutes until it all blends together. Pour out onto a work surface and continue kneading for a few minutes. The dough should be smooth and stretchy.

Folding & cooking

Roll out the dough into three logs. Cut into small 16–18 g (½ oz) pieces and cover with cling film (plastic wrap) or with a clean dish towel to stop the dough from drying out. Dust the work surface with flour and roll out the pieces of dough into 10 cm (4 in) discs. Use a pastry cutter to make perfect discs. Dollop a spoonful of filling onto the middle of each disc of dough. Fold like a Peking dumpling (page 142).

Cook in two batches or freeze some of the dumplings. Heat 2 tablespoons of oil in a 28 cm (11 in) non-stick lidded frying pan (skillet). Add half the dumplings, making sure they are not too close together; they should not be touching. Sizzle for a few minutes before adding water up to one-third of the height of the dumplings (around 220 ml/7½ fl oz). Cover with a lid and cook until the water has evaporated.

Uncover and toast the bottoms of the dumplings, check to see if they are cooked. They are done when they are nicely browned underneath. Repeat with the remaining dumplings, washing the pan in between each batch. Serve straight away.

Suggestion

You can serve these dumplings with crushed tomatoes. Dice 2 tomatoes. Add ¼ chopped onion and 2 chopped sprigs of flat-leaf parsley. Season and add 3 tablespoons of olive oil and 2 tablespoons of sherry vinegar.

DUMPLINGS
THREE-MUSHROOM
鮮菇素鍋貼

Makes **24 dumplings**
Soaking **1 night**
Preparation **45 mins**
Cooking **10 mins**

Filling
20 g (¾ oz) dried shiitake
   mushrooms
15 g (½ oz) dried wood ear
   mushrooms
250 g (9 oz) button
   mushrooms
1 large leek, white part only
   (180 g/6 oz)
3 garlic cloves
3 tbsp oil
2 tbsp oyster sauce
salt

Pastry
250 g (9 oz) strong white
   bread flour, plus extra for
   dusting
½ tsp salt
150 ml (5 fl oz) boiling water

Cooking
vegetable oil

Filling

The day before, soak the dried mushrooms in a large bowl of water. The next day, finely chop the shiitake and button mushrooms. Roughly chop the wood ear mushrooms, making sure you remove the hard parts. Chop the leek and press the garlic.

Heat the oil in a frying pan. Brown the leek and the shiitake and button mushrooms. Season lightly with salt. When the vegetables start to turn brown, add the oyster sauce, garlic and wood ear mushrooms. Continue cooking for just a minute. Taste and adjust the seasoning if necessary. Set aside.

Pastry

Combine the flour and salt in a large bowl and make a well in the centre. Pour in the boiling water, stirring with a spatula or chopsticks. When the pastry starts to turn lumpy, knead for 5 minutes until it all blends together. Pour it out onto a work surface and continue kneading for a few minutes. The pastry should be smooth and stretchy.

Folding

Roll out the dough into three logs. Cut into little 16–18 g (½ oz) pieces and cover with cling film (plastic wrap) or a clean dish towel to stop the dough from drying out. Dust the work surface with flour and roll out the pieces into 10 cm (4 in) discs. Use a pastry cutter to make perfect discs. Dollop a spoonful of filling onto the centre of each disc of dough, then fold like a Peking dumpling (page 142). Arrange the dumplings on a dish lined with baking parchment.

Cooking

Cook in two batches. Heat 2 tablespoons of vegetable oil in a 28 cm (11 in) non-stick lidded frying pan (skillet). Add half the dumplings to the pan, making sure they are not too close together; they should not be touching. Sizzle for a few minutes before adding water up to one-third of the height of the dumplings (around 220 ml (7½ fl oz)). Cover with a lid and cook until the water has evaporated. Uncover and toast the bottoms of the dumplings, checking to see if they are cooked. They are done when they are nicely browned underneath. Repeat with the remaining dumplings, washing the pan in between each batch. You can also steam-cook these dumplings for 8 minutes. Serve with a little soy sauce.

SIDES & SAUCES

SALAD
SMASHED CUCUMBER
涼拌拍黃瓜

Serves **4**
Preparation **20 mins**

2 cucumbers, ideally organic
6 coriander (cilantro) sprigs
2 spring onions (scallions)
  (optional)
1 tbsp toasted sesame seeds
coarse sea salt

Sauce
1 garlic clove
25 g (1 oz) fresh ginger root
1 small tsp Sichuan pepper
  and/or 1 dried chilli
30 g (1 oz/2½ tbsp) sugar
4 tbsp soy sauce
3 tbsp Chinkiang black rice
  vinegar
2 tbsp white rice vinegar
2 tbsp toasted sesame oil

Wash the cucumbers. Bash them with a rolling pin, turning by 90 degrees (quarter of a turn) each time. Cut into pieces. Remove any seeds that come away. Sprinkle with coarse sea salt. Stir and leave to drain in a colander while you make the sauce.

Press the garlic and finely slice the ginger. Crush the Sichuan pepper in a mortar or using a rolling pin. If you are adding a dried chilli pepper, remove the seeds. In a salad bowl, combine everything with the sugar, soy sauce, vinegars and sesame oil. Chop the coriander and spring onions (if using).

Quickly pat the cucumbers dry using a dish towel or paper towels. Transfer to a salad bowl. Add the herbs and mix together. Sprinkle with sesame seeds when it is time to serve.

AUBERGINES
BRAISED (HONG SHAO)
紅燒茄子

Serves **4**
Preparation **30 mins**
Cooking **25 mins**

500 g (1 lb 2 oz) aubergines
  (eggplants)
4 garlic cloves
30 g (1 oz) fresh ginger root
2 spring onions (scallions)/
  Asian chives
2 tbsp soy sauce
1 tbsp dark soy sauce
1 tbsp cane sugar
6 tbsp vegetable oil
salt and black pepper

Tip
The longer you drain the
aubergines, the less oil they
will absorb.

Chop the aubergines into even-sized pieces. Season generously with salt, mix and leave to drain in a colander while you prepare everything else.

Chop the garlic and slice the ginger. Chop the spring onions. Combine the soy sauces and sugar.

Heat the oil in a lidded frying pan (skillet). Pat the aubergines dry with paper towels and brown in the oil over a medium heat. When they are nicely browned, remove from the pan.

Brown the garlic and ginger. Add a little oil if necessary. Return the aubergines to the pan and add the sauce and 120 ml (4 fl oz) water. Season with pepper, reduce the heat to low, cover with a lid and cook for 10–15 minutes. Check if they are cooked by pricking with the end of a knife.The aubergines should be soft. Remove from the heat and add the spring onions.

ASIAN
SLAW
亞洲風味沙拉

Serves **6**
Preparation **20 mins**

½ red onion
2 carrots
¼ red cabbage
¼ tender white cabbage
 (e.g. pointed, Chinese,
 pontoise or cabus cabbage)
100 g (3½ oz) roasted and
 salted peanuts
½ bunch of coriander
 (cilantro)
4 spring onions (scallions)
 or Asian chives

Vinaigrette
5 tbsp maple syrup
3 tbsp soy sauce
5 tbsp sunflower oil
6 tbsp rice vinegar or cider
 vinegar
black pepper

Chop the onion and grate the carrots. Chop the cabbages as finely as possible, ideally using a vegetable slicer. Roughly chop the peanuts and coriander. Chop the spring onions. Combine all the salad ingredients. Mix together all the vinaigrette ingredients.

Pour the vinaigrette over the coleslaw and stir. Taste and adjust the seasoning if necessary. Serve straight away.

CHINESE CABBAGE SALAD

WITH SESAME SAUCE
涼拌白菜沙拉

Serves **4**
Preparation **15 mins**
Cooking **1 min 20 secs**

8 Chinese cabbage leaves
  (from the soft part)
250 g (9 oz) flat coco beans
4 tbsp sweet soy sauce
½ lemon
2 tbsp sesame oil
5 g (⅛ oz) fresh ginger root
1 small garlic clove (optional)
1 tsp black sesame seeds
salt

Chop the cabbage. Cut the flat beans in two lengthways, then slice crossways. Bring some salted water to the boil and cook the beans for 1 minute 20 seconds. Drop into cold water, then strain.

Grate the ginger, then press the garlic (if using). Combine with the soy sauce, sesame oil, and lemon juice.

Combine the vegetables, pour over the sauce and mix. Sprinkle with sesame seeds.

PANCAKE
SPRING ONION (CONG YOU BING)
蔥油餅

Makes **3 pancakes**
Preparation **35 mins**
Resting **40 mins**
Cooking **6 mins**

300 g (10½ oz) strong white
    bread flour, plus 30 g (1 oz)
    for dusting
1 level tsp salt
200 ml (7 fl oz) hot water
    (50–60°C/122–140°F)
1 tbsp vegetable oil + 3 tbsp
    for cooking
5 spring onions (scallions)
3 tbsp Chilli Oil (page 116)

Tips

Use a sieve (fine-mesh
strainer) to dust the flour
evenly over the pancakes.
If you don't have any chilli oil,
use vegetable oil instead.

Combine the flour and salt in a large bowl. Pour in the hot water a little at a time, stirring with a spatula or chopsticks. When the dough starts to turn lumpy, knead it for a good 5 minutes. It should be smooth and should not stick to your hands or to the bowl. Add a little flour if necessary. Shape into a ball. Grease the bowl with the 1 tablespoon vegetable oil and roll the ball of dough around inside to coat it in oil on all sides. Cover with cling film (plastic wrap) (in direct contact with the surface) and leave to rest for 40 minutes.

Finely chop the spring onions.

Weigh the dough and divide it into three portions. Cover with cling film to stop it from drying out. Dust the work surface with flour and roll out a piece of dough into a 35 x 25 cm (14 x 10 in) rectangle, as thinly as possible (page 152).

Brush the dough with 2 tablespoons of the chilli oil. Sprinkle with spring onions and dust with a little flour. Roll the long side over itself. Press down on the dough with your hands, pushing out any air. Stretch slightly, then roll it into the shape of a snail. Pull the end down under the snail to stop the pancake from unwrapping while cooking. Cover with cling film and leave to rest while you make the other pancakes.

Heat 1 tablespoon of oil in a frying pan. Gently roll out the snails so they are 3–5 mm (⅛–¼ in) thick. Dust with flour and cook the pancakes for 3 minutes on each side. Add more oil if needed. The pancakes should be golden brown and crisp. Enjoy them hot with some black vinegar sauce (page 118).

VEGETABLES
SAUTEED
什錦炒蔬菜

Serves **4–6**
Soaking **15 mins**
Preparation **15 mins**
Cooking **10 mins**

250 g (9 oz) mangetout
  (snow peas)
250 g (9 oz) bok choy
20 g (¾ oz) dried wood ear
  mushrooms
20 g (¾ oz) fresh ginger root
3 tbsp oyster sauce
3 garlic cloves
3 tbsp vegetable oil
black pepper

Soak the mushrooms in a large bowl of boiling water for 15 minutes. Chop the garlic. Slice the ginger.

Cut the bok choy into halves or quarters lengthways, depending on how long they are. Chop the mushrooms, removing the hard parts if necessary. Cut the largest mushrooms into pieces. Heat the oil in a wok or a large frying pan (skillet) over a very high heat and brown the garlic and ginger. Add the bok choy, mangetout and oyster sauce. Season with pepper, stir and cook for 2–3 minutes before adding the mushrooms. Continue cooking for 1–2 minutes. Taste and add a little salt if necessary. Sprinkle with 1 tablespoon of toasted sesame seeds before serving, if you wish.

KAI LAN
WITH FRIED GARLIC
蠔油芥蘭

Serves **4**
Preparation **15 mins**
Cooking **10 mins** for the garlic, **2 mins** for the vegetables

50 ml (1¾ fl oz/3 tbsp) vegetable oil
5 garlic cloves, chopped
400 g (14 oz) kai lan
2 tbsp oyster sauce
salt

Tip

You can substitute the kai lan with broccoli or bok choy.

Heat the oil in a small saucepan over a medium heat. Add the garlic, stirring occasionally, and cook until slightly browned. Turn off the heat and leave to cool. The garlic will continue cooking in the hot oil. Once it has cooled down, drain the garlic and save the flavoured oil for later.

Cut off the end of the stems and remove any damaged or discoloured leaves. Soak in water. Drain. If the stalks are too thick, cut them in half lengthways.

Make your sauce. Mix 4 tablespoons of the reserved garlic-flavoured oil and the oyster sauce together in a bowl. Add a tiny bit of salt. Stir and set aside.

Bring some water to the boil in a large saucepan. Add the kai lan and cook for 2 minutes. They should still be slightly crunchy. Drain, transfer to a salad bowl, add the sauce and stir. Serve straight away sprinkled with the sliced fried garlic.

FRIED RICE
WITH EGG & SPRING ONION
蛋炒飯

Serves **4**
Preparation **15 mins**
Cooking **10 mins**

1 small onion
5 spring onions (scallions)
500 g (1 lb 2 oz) cooked rice
  from the day before
  (280 g/10 oz uncooked rice)
2 tbsp oyster sauce
2 tbsp soy sauce
1 level tsp sugar
5 eggs
5 tbsp vegetable oil
small handful of chives
black pepper

Tips

The secret to making good
fried rice is to use cold rice.
Also, don't break the eggs
over the rice or it may
turn mushy.

Chop the onion and spring onions. Dress the cold rice with the sauces
and sugar. Season with pepper. Mix with your hands to separate the grains.
Break the eggs into a bowl, then season with salt and pepper. Heat
1 tablespoon of oil in a frying pan (skillet), then pour in the eggs. Cook
as you would for fried eggs then stir. Remove from the pan.

Pour in the rest of the oil, then add the onions. Cook for 3 minutes before
adding the rice. Season with pepper, stir and continue cooking until the
rice is hot and lightly browned. Return the eggs to the pan and mix. Add
the chives. Taste; adjusting the seasoning if necessary.

RADISH CAKE
WITH CHINESE SAUSAGE

蘿蔔糕

Serves **4–6**
Soaking **1 night**
Preparation **40 mins**
Cooking **40 mins**
Chilling **1 night**

800 g (1 lb 12 oz) white radish
100 g (3½ oz) rice flour
20 g (¾ oz) dried shiitake
  mushrooms
2 tbsp Maïzena®
2 Chinese sausages
4 spring onions (scallions),
  chopped
1 level tsp salt
1 level tsp sugar
black pepper
vegetable oil, for cooking

Rehydrate the shiitake mushrooms in a bowl of hot water, ideally the day before.

Peel and grate the daikon, then brown in a large dry frying pan (skillet), stirring occasionally. This will allow some of the water to evaporate. Transfer to a bowl and leave to cool.

Blanch the sausages in boiling water for 3 minutes then strain.

When the shiitake mushrooms are soft, remove the hard parts and chop finely. Dice the sausages. In the same frying pan, heat up 3 tablespoons of oil. Brown the mushrooms and the sausage for 5 minutes. Set aside.

Season the radish with the salt and sugar. Add generous amounts of pepper. Add the rice flour and Maïzena® and mix well. Add the garnish (mushrooms, sausages and spring onions) and stir. The mixture should be soft but not runny or hard. If it is too runny, add a little rice flour. If it is hard, this will mean the daikon is old, in which case add a little water.

Moisten a clean, thin dish towel and use to line a 19 cm (7½ in) bamboo basket, or a baking tin If you don't have one. Steam for 40 minutes (from the point at which the water comes to the boil).

Check to see if the cake is cooked by pricking it with a cocktail stick (toothpick): the centre should be firm. Leave to cool slightly before turning it over to remove from the tin. Leave to cool completely before cutting into slices. Ideally, cover with cling film (plastic wrap) and chill overnight.

The next day, heat up some oil in a frying pan. Cut the cake into 1 cm (½ in) slices and brown for 3–4 minutes on each side. Serve with some sriracha sauce (page 119).

You can eat the cake as soon as it is cooked if you prefer, but traditionally it is fried until golden brown first.

CHILLI OIL
WITH SICHUAN SPICES

四川紅油

Makes **1 jar**
Preparation **5 mins**
Cooking **10 mins**

10 g (¼ oz) Sichuan pepper
10 g (¼ oz) coriander seeds
3 star anise
1 cinnamon stick
5 large garlic cloves
45 g (1½ oz) chilli (hot pepper)
  flakes
220 ml (7½ fl oz) vegetable
  oil (e.g. peanut (groundnut),
  rapeseed (canola))

Pour the pepper into a large bowl.

Coarsely crush the Sichuan pepper, coriander seeds, star anise and cinnamon stick.

Using the side of a knife, crush the garlic on a cutting board. Add the garlic to a saucepan with the oil and the spices. Make sure you have a sieve to hand. Heat the oil over a very low heat. Stir frequently; don't let the spices burn. When the garlic starts to singe, use the sieve to pour the oil over the chilli pepper in three goes. Watch out for splashing. Leave to cool completely before transferring to a jar.

You can keep this oil in the refrigerator for several months.

You can add the garlic and some of the Sichuan pepper to the oil, as well as some coriander seeds. Avoid adding the cinnamon and star anise though, as they will taste unpleasant in your mouth and will be hard to remove once combined with other ingredients.

Tip

Make your own chilli mix depending on how strong you like it. For example, you could use one-third mild chilli, one-third Korean chilli powder for kimchi and one-third Thai or Chinese hot chilli.

SAUCE XO
XO醤

Makes **1 jar**
Soaking **1 night**
Preparation **35 mins**
Cooking **1 hr 40 mins**

25 g (1 oz) dried shiitake
  mushrooms
60 g (2 oz) dried prawns
  (shrimp)
60 g (2 oz) ham
4 shallots
5 large garlic cloves
15 g (½ oz) fresh ginger root
3 long red chillies
200 ml (7 fl oz) peanut
  (groundnut) oil
15 g (½ oz/1 tbsp) brown
  sugar
2 tbsp oyster sauce
3 tbsp soy sauce
1 tbsp Korean chilli powder
  (optional)
100 ml (3½ fl oz) Shaoxing
  wine

The day before, soak the shiitake mushrooms and prawns in a salad bowl filled with cold water. The next day, drain and reserve 100 ml (3⅓ oz) of the soaking water. Chop the shiitake and roughly chop the prawns using a knife.

Slice the ham into julienne strips. Chop the shallots, garlic and ginger. Remove the seeds from the chillies. Cut into big chunks.

Heat the oil in a frying pan (skillet) over a medium heat. Add the shallots, garlic and ginger. Brown for 5 minutes, stirring, add the prawns, mushrooms, ham and chillies.

Leave to simmer over a low heat for 10 minutes then add the seasonings, wine, and the soaking water reserved from earlier.

Cook over a low heat for 1 hour and 30 minutes. The liquid should have evaporated and the oil should have gently infused with the different flavours. Leave to cool before transferring to a jar.

The oil will protect the sauce, which can be kept in the refrigerator for up to 1 month. This sauce goes wonderfully with dumplings, noodles and white rice. Use the oil to sauté your wok dishes, such as vegetables, prawns, meat, rice, noodles, etc.

BLACK VINEGAR SAUCE
薑醋醬汁

Makes 1 small bowl
Preparation 10 mins

10 g (¼ oz) fresh ginger root
1 tsp brown sugar
2 tbsp Chinkiang black rice
  vinegar
2 tbsp soy sauce

Storage

The sauce can be kept in
the refrigerator for 1 week
(without the herbs).

Finely slice the ginger, then
cut into small cubes. Combine
the sugar with the vinegar
and soy sauce in a bowl. Add
the ginger.

You can serve this sauce with
dumplings or spring onion
pancakes.

Sprinkle with sesame seeds
or chopped herbs (e.g. chives,
coriander (cilantro), etc.) to
jazz it up a bit.

SAUCE COCONUT, MISO & LIME
味增椰奶醬

Makes 1 bowl
Preparation 5 mins
Cooking 3 mins

200 ml (7 fl oz) coconut milk
50 g (2 oz) white miso
15 g (¼ oz) fresh ginger root,
  grated
1 small organic lime

Storage

This sauce keeps
for 2 days.

Heat the coconut milk in a
small saucepan. Remove from
the heat and add the miso,
grated ginger, and lime juice
and zest. Whisk together.

Serve this sauce with salmon,
prawn or vegetable dumplings.

SAUCE DAN DAN

擔擔醬

Makes **1 bowl**
Preparation **5 mins**

80 g (3 oz) tahini
10 g (¼ oz/2½ tsp) sugar
50 ml (1¾ fl oz/3 tbsp) soy
  sauce
50 ml (1¾ fl oz/3 tbsp)
  Chinkiang black rice vinegar
chilli oil or chilli powder

Storage

This sauce can be kept in
the refrigerator for 1 week.

Mix the tahini with the sugar in
a bowl. Combine with the soy
sauce and vinegar.

Mix well before adding the
chilli oil or chilli powder.
Choose the strength of the
chilli according to your tastes.

This sauce goes particularly
well with grilled (broiled) pork
dumplings.

Shake the jar before using.

SAUCE SRIRACHA

是拉差辣椒醬

Makes **1 jar**
Preparation **5 mins**
Cooking **15 mins**

170 g (6 oz) long red chillies
50 g (2 oz) garlic
200 ml (7 fl oz) white rice
  vinegar
85 g (3 oz) brown sugar
1 heaped tsp salt
10 g (¼ oz/1 tbsp) Maïzena®

Storage

This sauce can be kept in
the refrigerator for 2 weeks.
Store in a jar wrapped in cling
film (plastic wrap) (in direct
contact with the sauce).

Cut the chillies in half
and remove the seeds.
Alternatively, slice the chillies
into rings and soak them in a
bowl filled with cold water –
this will make the seeds easier
to remove.

Peel the garlic. In a saucepan,
combine the chillies, vinegar,
sugar, salt and garlic. Bring
to the boil, reduce the heat,
then cook for 10 minutes. In a
bowl, mix the Maïzena® with a
little cold water. Pour into the
saucepan, stirring as you do
so, then leave to thicken.

Add the remaining raw
garlic clove and mix using a
hand-held blender or food
processor.

The mixture should be
smooth.

SWEET
SNACKS

BAO BUNS
COCONUT CREAM & TONKA BEAN
香豆椰奶包

Makes **12 bao buns**
Preparation **1 hr 30 mins**
Chilling **1 night**
Proofing **2 hours**
Cooking **15 mins**

Tonka & coconut cream
20 g (¾ oz/2¼ tbsp) strong
  white bread flour
30 g (1 oz) cornflour
  (cornstarch)
100 g (3½ oz) egg yolk
120 g (4 oz) brown sugar
2 tonka beans, finely grated
500 ml (17 fl oz) coconut milk

Extra-soft pastry
Mixture 1
265 g (9½ oz) strong white
  bread flour, sifted, plus
  extra for dusting
8 g (¼ oz/2 tsp) instant dried
  yeast
225 ml (8 fl oz) warm water
  (35°F/95°F)
Mixture 2
130 g (4½ oz) strong white
  bread flour, sifted
16.5 g (½ oz) baking powder
90 g (2½ oz) brown sugar
50 g (2 oz) melted butter

Tonka & coconut cream

Make the cream the day before. Combine the flour and cornflour in a large bowl. Whisk together the egg yolks, sugar and tonka beans in another large bowl. Bring the coconut milk to the boil in a pan. Mix half the milk with the egg yolks to thin them down. Return everything to the pan and boil for 2–3 minutes, stirring briskly with a whisk.

The cream needs to boil for a few minutes, otherwise it will be soft.

Transfer onto a plate. Wrap with cling film (plastic wrap) (in direct contact with the cream) and leave to cool before setting aside in the refrigerator until the following day.

Extra-soft pastry

Preheat the oven to its lowest possible setting. Combine the flour and yeast from mixture 1. Pour in the warm water, stirring with a whisk. Cover with a dish towel and leave to rest for 1 hour in the switched-off oven. The dough should form little bubbles and double in volume.

Cut out 12 squares of baking parchment measuring 6–7 cm (2½–2¾ in) on each side.

Combine the flour, baking powder, and sugar from mixture 2 in a larger bowl. Pour into mixture 1 a little at a time, stirring by hand. Add the cold melted butter and continue stirring. When the dough is smooth and even, pour it out onto a floured work surface and knead with the palm of your hand until it no longer sticks to your hands. Add more flour if necessary.

Folding & cooking

Weigh the dough. Roll it out into a log, then divide into 12 balls.

Weigh the cream and divide into 12 portions, then roughly shape into balls. Roll out the balls of dough, dollop one ball of cream on top and start making your bao buns (page 132).

Arrange each bun on a square of baking parchment. Cover with a dish towel and leave to rise for 1 hour in a warm place.

Pour a good amount of water into a steamer. Add the buns, making sure they are nicely spaced apart as they will rise while cooking. When the water comes to the boil, reduce the heat slightly and add the baskets. Cook for 15 minutes. Remove the buns with a spatula and repeat with the rest.

Enjoy warm.

These buns can be kept in the refrigerator for four to five days. To reheat, simply steam for 10 minutes.

DUMPLINGS
COCONUT CARAMEL
焦糖椰奶餃

Makes **30 dumplings**
Preparation **40 mins**
Cooking **4–5 mins**

Coconut caramel
200 g (7 oz) sugar
2 tbsp water
50 ml (1¾ fl oz/3 tbsp)
  coconut milk
250 g (9 oz) (available in
  Asian grocery stores)

Fruit salad
1 large ripe mango
4 passion fruits
1 organic lime

Pastry
1 packet of gyoza wrappers,
  defrosted if necessary

Coconut caramel

Make your caramel by heating the sugar in a frying pan (skillet) with the water. When the caramel turns a nice amber colour, pour in the coconut milk. Bring to the boil, then add the grated coconut. Stir. Pour into a container and leave to cool.

Fruit salad

Finely dice the mango, add to a bowl and mix with the flesh of the passion fruit. Add the lime zest and a dash of juice.

Keep in the refrigerator.

Folding & cooking

Separate the discs of dough, defrosted in advance if necessary (you can buy them fresh, but they are quite hard to find). Add a spoonful of coconut caramel. Moisten the edges and start folding like Peking dumplings (page 142) or in the shape of a fan (page 138).

Arrange in cooking baskets lined with baking paper. Bring the steamer water to the boil before adding the baskets. Cook for 4–5 minutes. Leave to cool for 2 minutes. Serve the dumplings, add the fruit salad and top with juice.

HAZELNUT CHOCOLATE
& RED KIDNEY BEAN BAO BUNS
紅豆榛果巧克力包

Makes **10 bao buns**
Preparation **1 hr**
Chilling **1 night**
Proofing **2 hrs**
Cooking **15 mins**

Bean, hazelnut & chocolate cream

200 g (7 oz) tinned red kidney
   beans, drained
80 g (3 oz) hazelnut paste
   (from an organic food store)
150 g (5 oz) good-quality dark
   chocolate (66 per cent
   cocoa)
150 ml (5 fl oz) plant-based
   beverage (e.g. hazelnut, oat,
   coconut, almond)
50 ml (1¾ fl oz/3 tbsp) maple
   syrup

Traditional pastry

8 g (¼ oz/2 tsp) instant dried
   yeast
165 ml (5½ fl oz) water
300 g (10½ oz) sugar
300 g (10½ oz) strong white
   bread flour, sifted
pinch of salt
1 tsp bicarbonate of soda
   (baking soda) (optional)
1½ tbsp vegetable oil

Tip

If you did not make your
cream the day before, place
the dish in the freezer for
40 minutes so you can still
shape it into balls.

Bean, hazelnut & chocolate cream

The day before, roughly chop the chocolate. Melt in a heatproof bowl
set over a pan of hot water or in the microwave. Combine all the other
ingredients using a food processor or hand-held blender. Add the melted
chocolate and mix until nice and smooth. Transfer to a dish. Wrap in cling
film (plastic wrap) (in direct contact with the surface) and keep in the
refrigerator until the next day.

The next day, divide the cream into 10 portions. Roughly shape into balls
by hand to make it easier to assemble your buns.

Keep chilled.

Traditional pastry

Preheat the oven to its lowest setting. Mix the yeast, warm water and sugar
together in a bowl. In a container, combine the flour, salt and bicarbonate
of soda. Make a well in the centre, then the oil then pour in the water
mixture. Mix with chopsticks or with the ends of your fingers. When the
dough starts to turn lumpy, start kneading. All the flour needs to have been
absorbed. Pour out onto the work surface and continue kneading until the
dough is smooth and even. It should not stick to your hands. Shape into a
ball, cover with a clean dish towel and leave to rise for 1 hour the switched-
off oven or in a warm place. The dough should double in volume. Cut out
squares of baking parchment measuring 6–7 cm (2½–2¾ in)on each side.

Folding & cooking

Weigh the pastry and divide into 10 pieces. Shape into balls, then roll out
the pieces of dough into 13–14 cm (5–5½ in) discs (page 132). The edges
should be thinner than the centres. Spoon a ball of cream onto each disc
and fold like a bao bun. You can keep the folds on top or turn the bao buns
over so the top is nice and smooth.

Place each bun on a square of baking parchment, then arrange in steamer
baskets. Make sure they are well spaced apart as the buns will rise while
cooking. Cover with a dish towel and leave to rise for 1 hour in a warm
place.

Pour a good amount of water into a steamer. When the water comes to
the boil, reduce the heat slightly and add the baskets. Cook for 15 minutes.
Remove the buns with a spatula and repeat with the remaining buns. You
can dust your bao buns with unsweetened cocoa powder. Leave to cool
for 10 minutes then tuck in!

TWISTED BAO BUNS
WITH COCONUT OIL & BLACK SESAME SEEDS
甜花捲

Makes **16 twisted bao buns**
Preparation **1 hr**
Proofing **1 hr 40 mins**
Cooking **15 mins**

Extra-soft pastry
Mixture 1
265 g (9½ oz) strong white
  bread flour, sifted, plus
  extra for dusting
8 g (¼ oz/2 tsp) instant dried
  yeast
225 ml (8 fl oz) warm water
  (35°F/95°F)
Mixture 2
130 g (4½ oz) strong white
  bread flour
16.5 g (½ oz) baking powder
75 g (2½ oz) brown sugar
30 g (1 oz) sesame seeds
40 g (1½ oz) melted butter

Decoration
120 g (4 oz) coconut oil
100 g (3½ oz) brown sugar
  (e.g. vergeoise or
  muscovado)

Tip
If you have some large
steamer baskets or several
medium-sized ones, place
the buns inside to allow them
to rise.

Decoration and extra-soft pastry

Heat the coconut oil to liquefy it then mix with 100 g (3½ oz) brown sugar. Leave to cool completely, stirring occasionally. It should have the texture of softened butter.

Preheat the oven to 30°C. Combine the flour and yeast from mixture 1. Pour in the warm water, stirring with a whisk. Cover with a dish towel and leave to rest for 1 hour in the switched-off oven. The dough should form bubbles and double in size.

Cut out 16 squares of baking parchment measuring 6–7 cm (2½–2¾ in) on each side.

Combine the flour, baking powder, sesame seeds, and sugar from mixture 2. Pour into mixture 1 a little at a time, stirring by hand. Add the cold melted butter and continue to mix.

When the dough is even, pour it out onto a floured work surface and knead with the palm of your hand until it no longer sticks to your hands. Add more flour if needed. Roll out the dough into a 38 x 30 cm (15–12 in) rectangle.

Folding & cooking

Pour the coconut oil and sugar mixture onto the dough, then roll out as evenly as possible using a spatula. If there is no decoration in some places, folding will help make sure there is some on each bun.

Fold the dough in three (page 134). Then cut into 16 segments and twist. Place each twisted bao bun on a square of baking parchment and leave to rise for 40 minutes at room temperature.

Place in steamer baskets; make sure the buns are well spaced apart as the buns will rise will cooking. Bring the water in the steamer to the boil. Reduce the heat slightly and add the baskets.

Cook for 15 minutes. Enjoy warm.

TECHNICAL
MANUAL

SIMPLE
BAO BUN FOLD

1

Roll out your ball of dough. When it starts to take on a round shape, roll out the edges some more so it is slightly thicker in the centre.

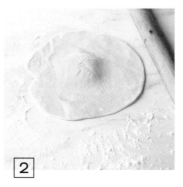

2

You need to produce a disc with a diameter of 15 cm (6 in).

3

Drop the ball of filling onto the centre, where the dough is at its thickest.

4

Take hold of one edge of the dough with your thumb and index finger (right hand if you are right-handed) and fold.

5

With your other index finger, make another fold and pinch with your right thumb and index finger to seal it to the first fold. Don't move your right thumb – it should be holding the first fold in place at all times.

6

Continue making folds as you turn the bao bun over, keeping your right thumb on the first fold at all times.

7

t the end, you should be holding all he folds between your right thumb and ndex finger.

8

Close up the bun by turning it over and pinching the centre. Make a small ball to seal it up.

9

If the dough seems too thick, cut a bit off with some scissors. Don't overdo it though! Place the buns on squares of baking parchment and leave to rise.

FOLD
TWISTED BAO BUN

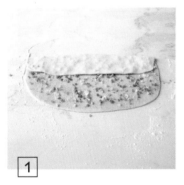

1

Dust the work surface with flour
and roll out your bao bun dough
into a rectangle measuring 40 x 30 cm
(16 x 12 in). Add the garnish.

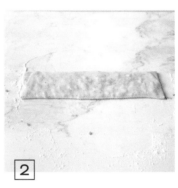

2

Fold the dough in three lengthways,
starting at the top, then fold the bottom.
The layers of dough should
be overlapping at the edges.

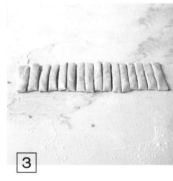

3

Cut the rectangle in half. Then cut each
half in half again, and so on. At the end,
you should have 16 more or less equally
sized strips of dough.

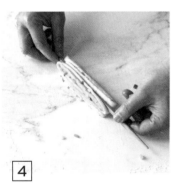

4

Place two strips of dough on top of
each other. Take a chopstick and
press into the centre of the two strips
(lengthways).

5

Turn the dough over so that the smooth
side is on top and roll the strip out a
little to make it bigger.

6

Place the chopstick in the middle of the
strip, on the smooth side. Take hold of
the edges of the dough. The chopstick
should be facing downwards.

7

Twist the chopstick. Then turn the bao bun over so the chopstick is at the top.

8

Lay it out on the work surface with the edges underneath the dough. Press down, then remove the chopstick. Arrange on a square of baking parchment.

Tip

If it helps to visualise it, the process could be likened to the act of styling your hair into a bun with a hair stick. You twist your hair round, then insert the stick to hold the bun in place. The principle is the same for twisted bao buns, except that you remove the chopstick at the end.

FOLD
HAR GAO OR HAKAO FOLD

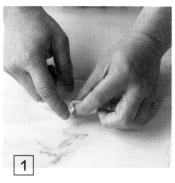

1

Using your thumb and index finger, take hold of one edge of the dough on the top part of the disc. Make a fold with the index finger of your other hand. Pinch to seal together.

2

Make eight more folds in the same way, continuing in the same direction.

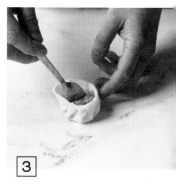

3

This will create a small bag, with a smooth part and a folded part. Add a spoonful of filling up against the folds; be careful not to overfill and make sure you leave a little border of dough so you can close up the dumpling.

4

Seal up the dumpling by folding the smooth part of the dough down over the folds.

5

Press down and pinch the dough together to seal it.

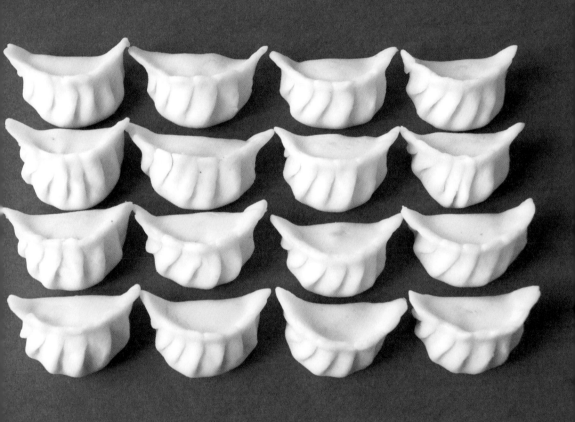

FOLD
BAG + FAN FOLD

1 Moisten the edges of a square wonton wrapper using a pastry brush. Dollop one spoonful of filling onto the centre.

2 Take hold of two opposite corners (diagonally) with your thumb and index finger.

3 With your other hand, pull the sides of the dough towards the centre and squeeze the filling in the palm of your hand, pressing down on the dough with your thumb to seal it up. Imagine you are trying to pack the filling into the dough.

1 Moisten the edges of a round gyoza pastry wrapper with a pastry brush. If you are using homemade dough, there is no need to moisten it. Dollop a spoonful of filling onto the centre.

2 Close up the dumpling into a half moon, pushing out the air as you do so.

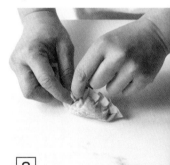

3 Place the dumpling in front of you horizontally, with the closure facing upwards, and make some folds resembling gathers in the same direction.

FOLD
THREE-CORNERED HAT + PYRAMID FOLD

1

Dollop a little of the filling onto the centre of the disc of dough.

2

Pinch two edges of the dough together as if to form the tip of a triangle. Stop at the centre of the dumpling.

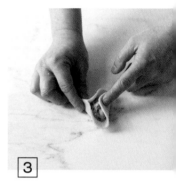

3

Hold onto the tip of the triangle with your thumb and index finger (same hand). Then pull down the dough on the opposite side with the index finger of your other hand. This will create a three-cornered hat. Pinch firmly to close up the three edges of the dough.

1

Dollop a little of the filling onto the centre of your disc of dough. You should add less filling to these dumplings.

2

Pinch two edges of the dough together and close them up in the centre using your thumb and index finger (of the same hand).

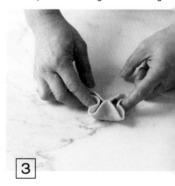

3

Make two other folds in the other direction. Pinch firmly to seal the four edges of the dough together.

FOLD
PEKING DUMPLING

1

Dollop one spoon of filling onto the centre of a disc of dough.

2

Join together the two edges of the dough facing you in the centre; pinch with your thumb and index finger.

3

With your other index finger, make a fold near the middle, where you are pinching.

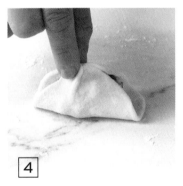

4

Let go of the centre with your fingers and pinch the fold to seal it up well.

5

Make three to four more folds in the same direction, following the same instructions.

6

When you reach the edge, pinch the dough firmly to seal up the edge. Start again from the centre and fold in the other direction.

FOLD
FISH OR TORTELLINI

1

Moisten the edges of a square wonton wrapper using a pastry brush.

2

Add a spoonful of the filling.

3

Seal up the dumpling by joining togethe two corners and pushing the air out. This will create a triangle.

4

Pick up the dumpling in your hand and place your index finger in the middle of the filling side, with the tip facing you. Press down slightly to mark the middle – this will make it easier to fold.

5

Moisten the two side tips.

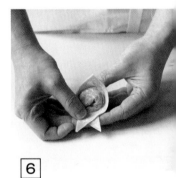

6

Join together the two tips by crossing them to form a fish tail or V shape. Press down to seal up the dough. You can make this fold with round pastry dough.

FOLD
LEAF

1

Add a spoonful of filling in the shape of a small quenelle, facing you. The filling should be arranged vertically, rather than horizontally as with other dumplings.

2

Pinch the dough at the bottom, creating a 2 cm (¾ in) tip.

3

Push the tip inside the disc, against the filling, and join up the two side edges of the dough. Pinch to seal and to form a new tip.

4

Push the tip inside again, and pull the side edges together, creating a new tip each time.

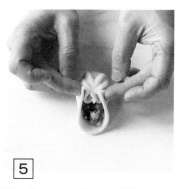

5

This will create a plaited (braided) effect. To ensure the dumpling is watertight, make sure the dough you pull down is fully wrapped around the tip.

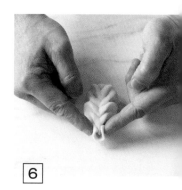

6

Continue plaiting (braiding) before sealing up the dumpling by pinching the final tip.

FOLD
SOUP BAO BUN OR DUMPLING

1

Dollop a spoonful of jelly soup filling onto the centre of a disc of dough.

2

Take hold of one edge of the dough with your thumb and index finger. Using your other index finger too, make a fold.

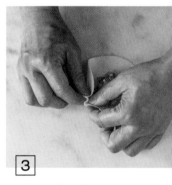

3

Continue making folds in the same direction.

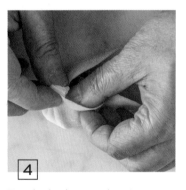

4

Turn the dough over and continue making folds (in the shape of an accordion).

5

Use your other thumb (the left one if you are right-handed) to push the filling inside the dumpling. Make the final fold by gathering the dough in the middle and turn over to close.

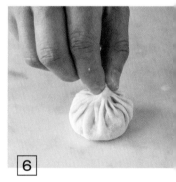

6

Make a little tip on the top so you can pick it up without breaking it. If the tip is too thick, cut off any excess dough with some scissors, then make a new tip.

Tip
As these dumplings or bao buns are fragile, keep them in the freezer on a dish lined with baking paper while you finish making the others.

PASTRY
TWO-COLOURED

1

Pour the boiling hot, coloured water into the centre of the well and stir with chopsticks or a spatula.

2

Mix until the dough starts to turn lumpy.

3

Blend the lumps by hand. The dough may seem dry but you need to continue kneading.

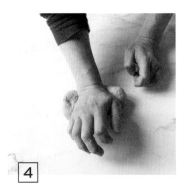

4

Pour it out onto a work surface and knead for 5 minutes with the palm of your hand. The dough should be stretchy and smooth. Repeat with the white dough. When the dough is ready, cover with cling film (plastic wrap) to stop it from drying out.

5

Roll out the coloured dough into a log measuring 26 cm (10½ in) long and roll out the white dough into a rectangle measuring 28 x 16 cm (11 x 6¼) in.

6

Wrap the pink log in the white dough, creating a roll.

7

Cut the roll in half. Roll out each log to reduce the diameter to 2.5-3 cm (1-1¼ in). Cut into 18-20 g (¾ oz) pieces. Wrap in cling film.

8

Dust the work surface and roll out the pieces of dough into discs with a diameter of 10-12 cm (4-4½ in).

9

Use a pastry cutter to create perfect discs. Make all your discs before you begin folding. Dust with plenty of flour to stop them from sticking and wrap in cling film.

PANCAKE
SPRING ONION

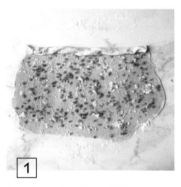

1

Dust the work surface with flour and roll out the dough into a 35 x 25 cm (14 x 10 in) rectangle, as thinly as possible. Add the garnish.

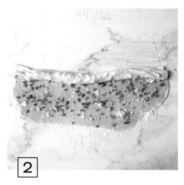

2

Roll the long side over itself to create a roll.

3

Compress the roll by pressing down with your hands and pushing the air out Stretch out the roll slightly, then roll into a snail shape.

4

Pull the end down under the snail to stop the pancake from coming apart while cooking. Cover with cling film (plastic wrap) and leave to rest while you make the rest of your snails.

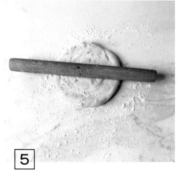

5

When you are ready to start cooking, heat your frying pan (skillet) and carefully roll out the snails so they are 3–5 mm (⅛–¼ in) thick. Dust with flour if necessary.

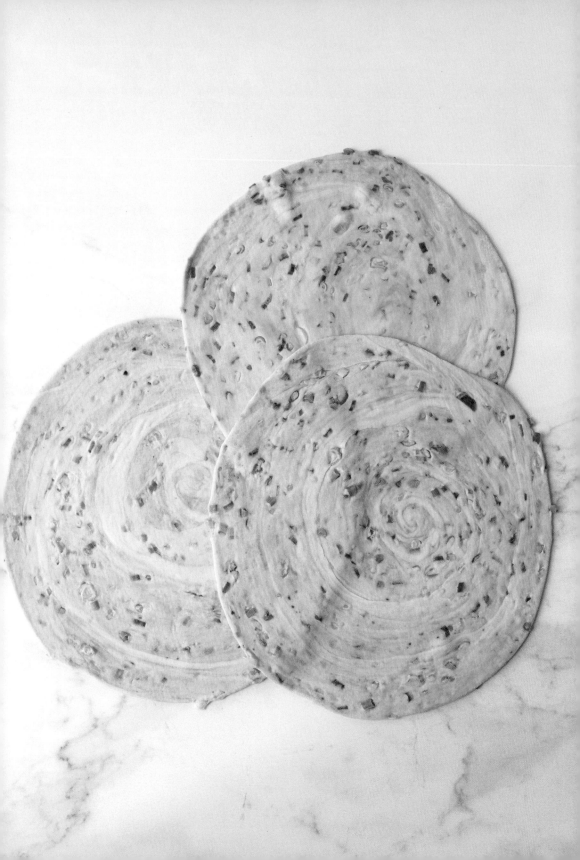

LIST
OF RECIPES

INDEX

Sesame (seeds)

Twisted bao buns with coconut oil & black sesame seeds — 128
Baked char siu bao buns — 42
Chinese cabbage salad & sesame sauce — 104
Smashed cucumber salad — 98

Sesame oil

Beef, sesame & celery dumplings — 78
Chinese cabbage with sesame sauce — 104

Shiitake mushrooms

Mama's minced pork & baby vegetable bao buns — 16
Radish cake with Chinese sauce — 114
Tofu, boy choy & shiitake bao buns — 30
3-mushroom dumplings — 94
Veggie carrot, kohlrabi & shiitake dumplings — 52
Veggie tofu, carrot, mushroom & kimchi dumplings — 84
XO sauce — 117

Sichuan pepper

Duck, mushroom & five-spice bao buns — 20
Spiced pulled pork bao buns — 24
Chilli oil with Sichuan spices — 116
Prawn, celeriac & Sichuan pepper dumplings — 54
Dumplings with pork, Sichuan pepper & dan dan sauce — 76
Smashed cucumber salad — 98

Smoked duck breast fillet

Mushroom & smoked duck breast fillet dumplings — 66

Spinach

Chicken, spinach & wood ear mushroom money bags — 82
Two-coloured bao buns with coppa & sundried tomatoes — 34
Vegetable curry bao buns — 28
Tofu, bok choy & shiitake bao buns — 30
Cod, ginger & spring onion dumplings — 58
Salmon, miso & ginger dumplings — 56

Spring onion

Twisted bao buns with spring onion (hua juan) — 32
Cod, ginger & spring onion dumplings — 58
Spring onion pancake (cong you bing) — 106
Fried rice with egg & spring onion — 112

Sundried tomatoes

Two-coloured bao buns with coppa & sundried tomatoes — 34

T

Tahini

Dan dan sauce — 119

Tofu

Tofu, bok choy & shiitake bao buns — 30
Veggie tofu, carrot, mushroom & kimchi dumplings — 84

Tonka beans

Coconut cream & tonka bean bao buns — 122

W

Water chestnuts

Mama's minced pork & baby vegetable bao buns — 16
Pork shumai (xiu mai) — 62
Crab dumplings with coconut & lemongrass soup — 70
Fried prawn dumplings — 68

White cabbage

Asian slaw — 102

White miso

Salmon, miso & ginger dumplings — 56
Coconut, miso & lime sauce — 118

White rice vinegar

Sriracha sauce — 119

Wood ear mushrooms

Golden chicken money bags — 72
Chicken, spinach & wood ear mushroom money bags — 82
Mama's minced pork & baby vegetable bao buns — 16
Tofu, bok choy & shiitake bao buns — 30
Half-moon dumplings with pork & wood ear mushrooms (fun guo) — 50
Sautéed vegetables — 108
3-mushroom dumplings — 94

Y

Young coconut

Coconut caramel dumplings — 124

First published in 2021 by Hachette Livre (Marabout)
This edition published in 2023 by Hardie Grant Books,
an imprint of Hardie Grant Publishing

Hardie Grant Books (London)
5th & 6th Floors
52–54 Southwark Street
London SE1 1UN

Hardie Grant Books (Melbourne)
Building 1, 658 Church Street
Richmond, Victoria 3121

hardiegrantbooks.com

British Library Cataloguing-in-Publication Data. A
catalogue record for this book is available from the
British Library.

Bao and Dim Sum
ISBN: 978-1-78488-574-8
10 9 8 7 6 5 4 3 2 1

For Hardie Grant:
Publishing Director: Kajal Mistry
Acting Publishing Director: Emma Hopkin
Senior Editor: Eila Purvis
Translator: Victoria Weavil
Typesettor: David Meikle
Proofreader: Kathy Steer
Production Controller: Sabeena Atchia

For Marabout:
Proofreading: Natacha Kotchetkova
Layout: Olivier Van Bellighen

Colour reproduction by p2d
Printed and bound in China by Leo Paper Products Ltd.